'They Say'

New Narratives in American History

Series Editors
James West Davidson
Michael B. Stoff

'They Say'

Ida B. Wells
and the Reconstruction of Race

James West Davidson

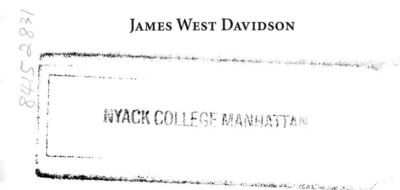
OXFORD
UNIVERSITY PRESS

2009

OXFORD
UNIVERSITY PRESS

Oxford University Press, Inc., publishes works that further
Oxford University's objective of excellence
in research, scholarship, and education.

Oxford   New York
Auckland   Cape Town   Dar es Salaam   Hong Kong   Karachi
Kuala Lumpur   Madrid   Melbourne   Mexico City   Nairobi
New Delhi   Shanghai   Taipei   Toronto

With offices in
Argentina   Austria   Brazil   Chile   Czech Republic   France   Greece
Guatemala   Hungary   Italy   Japan   Poland   Portugal   Singapore
South Korea   Switzerland   Thailand   Turkey   Ukraine   Vietnam

Published by Oxford University Press, Inc.
198 Madison Avenue, New York, New York 10016
www.oup.com

Library of Congress Cataloging-in-Publication Data
Davidson, James West.
They say : Ida B. Wells and the reconstruction of race / James West Davidson.
p. cm.—(New narratives in American history)
Includes bibliographical references and index.
ISBN-13: 978-0-19-516020-8 (cloth : alk paper)—ISBN-13: 978-0-19-516021-5 (pbk. : alk paper)
1. Wells-Barnett, Ida B., 1862-1931.   2. Wells-Barnett, Ida B., 1862-1931–Childhood and
youth.   3. African American women civil rights workers–Biography.   4. Civil rights
workers–United States–Biography.   5. African American women social reformers–United
States–Biography.   6. African American women educators–Biography.   7. African
Americans–Race identity.   8. African Americans–Social conditions–To 1964.   9. Racism–
United States–History–19th century.   10. United States–Race relations–History–
19th century.   I. Title.

E185.97.W55D385   2007
323.092–dc22
[B]

2007004756

9 8 7 6 5 4 3 2 1

Printed in the United States of America
on acid-free paper

For Mary

a painter whose mastery of negative space in a positive way
has pushed me to be a more truthful observer

Contents

FOREWORD

WHAT MAKES A LIFE? WHAT GIVES IT SHAPE AND TEXTURE—AN identity? Do we define ourselves or does what the world tells us—what *they say*—define who we are? James West Davidson has chosen to answer these questions with the gripping story of the first thirty years of the life of Ida B. Wells. More than one biographer has written about Wells, the African American teacher, journalist, and activist, and her battle against the scourge of lynching. None has focused exclusively on these years, largely before she took up the antilynching crusade. Why should we?

The answer lies in the title of Davidson's book, *'They Say': Ida B. Wells and the Reconstruction of Race*. Davidson chronicles Wells's early life within the fluid context of one of the most important episodes in American history: the first, formative steps in freedom of some four million, newly liberated slaves. Wells was born into slavery in 1862, within days of the announcement of Lincoln's Emancipation Proclamation. When freedom came three years later, former slaves struggled to reconstruct their identities as independent men and women.

It is their story that we see in the lives of Wells and her family. We follow her parents, James and Elizabeth, as they raise their children: he taking an interest in politics as a "race man" to ensure that African Americans ran for (and won) political office, she presiding over the household and instilling in her children the middle-class Victorian values of religion, modesty, morality, and self-discipline.

Those parental strands—of political activism and Victorian propriety—were woven together in Wells as they were in many African Americans emerging from bondage. The two strands did not always entwine easily, as young Ida discovered when she found herself summarily ejected from a segregated railroad car. The primly dressed Wells, the very model of a Victorian lady, fought back in a most unladylike way as the conductor attempted to dislodge her from her seat. Middle-class woman of modesty or militant activist? Proud black woman or insolent virago? She says or *they say?* This reciprocal, interactive process of self-definition and definition by others tells us much about blacks and whites as racial identities and race relations were being formed and reformed during Reconstruction and its aftermath.

As the color line separating blacks and whites was drawn ever more starkly and the socially constructed definition of race spelled out with greater and greater specificity, Wells rebelled, not only against whites eager to tell her who she was and what she could (and could not) do but against blacks who refused to resist the growing caste system embedded in such boundaries and definitions. In Davidson's hands, Wells's famous crusade against lynching becomes the culmination, not the commencement, of who she was.

The Germans call this genre *bildungsroman,* loosely meaning a story of development or education. Wells's struggle to define herself, however, is much more than the story of personal development. It is also a bildungsroman of the often-violent confrontation between whites and blacks in the post-emancipation world of nineteenth-century America, where color was a matter of contestation and race mattered more than ever. And it is a bildungsroman of middle-class women—black and white—defining themselves in a world where gender, too, was being contested and reconstructed and mattered as much as ever. Davidson's narrative choice of bildungsroman to tell these formative stories thus makes '*They Say*' a valuable addition to the Oxford New Narratives in American History, which seeks fresh approaches to reconstructing the story of American life as it was lived.

Michael B. Stoff
Series Coeditor

Acknowledgments

In a book centered on self-definition, I owe thanks to friends and colleagues who were kind enough to read all or portions of the manuscript to help me define the shape of this book. They include Christine Heyrman, Loren Schweninger, John Rugge, and Katherine Cress. Other scholars reviewed the manuscript for Oxford and provided valuable reactions, including Melissa Anyiwo at the University of Tennessee at Chattanooga, Judith Giesberg at Villanova University, Rachel Goosen at Washburn University, and Jennifer Ritterhouse at Utah State University. I made ample use of their generous insights. Thanks are also due to the staffs of the Memphis Public Library and the libraries of Vassar College and Yale University for helping me track down materials.

Having written a book centered on Ida B. Wells, I must say directly how much I am indebted to the scholars who have already followed these paths. Alfreda M. Duster, Wells's youngest daughter, shepherded her mother's autobiography into print, sparking a much-needed reexamination of a life so fully lived. Miriam

DeCosta-Willis superbly annotated and published the Memphis diary, providing a key to Wells's many acquaintances. More recently Linda O. McMurry and Patricia A. Schechter have written detailed studies of Wells that illuminate both her personality and her contributions to the reform movements of her time. My own work could not have proceeded without theirs.

Above all I owe a debt of gratitude to Michael B. Stoff, my coeditor on the New Narratives series at Oxford and the editor of this book. Mike was an ideal colleague from start to finish. He tendered invaluable advice on the small details as well as the broader picture. A more patient listener and incisive critic would be hard to imagine.

Thanks also are due to Chris Rogers and Peter Coveney, the former for encouraging me to launch New Narratives and the latter for listening as I bounced ideas off him for this volume. Peter was also instrumental in giving the series its handsome design. Though both have moved on to new positions, their enthusiasm for the project persists. Those who replaced them, John Challice and Brian Wheel, have been most encouraging and helpful. Finally my wife, Mary Untalan, has supported me throughout my labors with patience and good cheer, as have my children, Ella and Angus—especially when I was ungrateful enough to disappear, like some wraith into a time machine, upward into the attic and the books.

If I am not who you say I am,
then you are not who you think you are.

—James Baldwin

"Dose This Look Natchel?"

✦—✦

T HERE WAS A BOAT AT LEAST. G. H. FARNUM MANAGED THAT.

Did he commandeer somebody to row him out to the middle of the river and steady the craft against the current? Perhaps he handled the business himself, dropping an anchor to keep the boat in position. Certainly he was a professional. Already in his career Farnum had taken nigh well onto three thousand photographs and owned a studio of his own in Okemah, Oklahoma.

The problem was one of technique: how to get everybody in the picture. There were some fifty people standing around the bridge over the Canadian River. Getting them all in meant moving back, and a view from midstream was clearly the solution.

The day was May 25, 1911. A light breeze rippled the river. From this distance, the camera did not catch much detail on faces. But the clothing alone betrayed a remarkably wide social range: the well-to-do and humble, rural farmers in overalls as well as city folks in ties and jackets, young children, teenagers, and older men. All come out on a Thursday.

At the far left several women boasted stylish skirts and blouses, as well as hats to keep off the sun. Farther to the right, below the

umbrella, a mother held her infant, while just down the line, a little girl perched on a rail. It's hard to tell, she may be barefoot.

Even if the faces were too distant to fathom, the body language was easier to make out. The most confident figure—two thirds of the way to the right,—sported a stylish hat, vest, and a well-tailored coat. His stance was secure: feet apart, one hand in his pocket, the other holding one of the bridge's steel cables. Several younger folk posed jauntily, holding onto a strut, or standing up on a railing. Everyone waited patiently as Farnum set up.

How many would want to buy a copy of the photo? Hard to tell, but there would be good business in it. Certainly Farnum could use the money. His wife had given birth to a young son only two months earlier, so there was another mouth to feed at home.[1] But he was not just taking a picture. He was making this photo into a postcard, and postcards were good business.

In 1898, the post office had put into effect the low rate of a penny postage for what it called "private mailing cards," stock with an illustration or photo on one side and an address and stamp on the other. For the cost of the card and a penny stamp, a vacationing family could

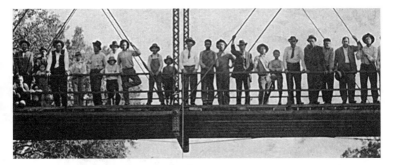

report to relatives on the good times they were enjoying. Hotels sold pastel-tinted likenesses of their establishments, while amusement parks like Coney Island trumpeted their most thrilling rides. Out of civic pride, cities produced cards of main streets with bustling trolleys; and, out of pride, their citizens bought and sent them.

Enterprising photographers took this idea a step further. Eastman Kodak began selling film designed to be turned into postcards, with the necessary address lines and *stamp here* printed on the back. Thus anyone who could take a picture could make a postcard. As the fad spread, even ordinary folk jumped into the business. "I have known blacksmiths and cobblers [and even dentists] to double up with it," commented one rueful photographer, "so it was possible to have a horse shod, your boots tapped, a tooth pulled, or a likeness taken by the same man." Not much capital was needed to set up. One Cincinnati photographer got his start by having an assistant collect fees from the customers lined up outside his shop, then running off to buy film.

For those in the picture, the act of being captured on film was still novel enough to retain an element of mystery and excitement. "I looked forward to having my picture taken weeks ahead," recalled one woman years later. "I tried to decide which side was my best, right or left…and I knew that soon I would mail myself off in all my glory to my loved ones. I was nervous. I thought the camera could *catch* me…I would be stopped for one moment and then I would be off in the mails, not to be retrieved again." In myriad towns across the nation, the camera did catch people who wished to see and be seen. This young man in Troy, Kansas (above), who promised a full letter to his sister once "picnic week" was over, could not resist scribbling a last-minute postscript in the upper left corner, asking whether his portrait looked natural. ("Dose this look natchel?")

The vacationing Alice Hobbs (on the following page) was concerned that she looked *un*natural from the wind.

With faster film, photographers were able to capture more candid scenes. Yet if the settings became more informal, the act of

On the Bear Camp River, at Osipee Valley.

The wind blew my hair so that it does not look natural.

picture taking remained deliberate. Indeed, postcard photography was doubly intentional, involving as it did not only a decision to be in the photo, but also to send it into the world, "stopped for one moment and then off in the mails." The act of being photographed was a conscious one, an act of self-definition.[2]

So it was for the Oklahoma folk lining up for G. H. Farnum along the Canadian River. The people on the bridge at Okemah spread out side by side, so that no one's view was blocked. Almost everyone looked at the camera, except for a few folk, like the man in the bow tie standing just to the left of the three girls. He is looking downward. So is the man to the left.

Farnum maneuvered the boat until he was finally ready—back far enough to be able to capture the entire expanse of river. Far enough, certainly, so that he could not miss what he came to photograph, and what everyone was looking at, before they stopped to arrange themselves to have their picture taken.

-1911-
COPYRIGHT
G.H.RAYNUM -2897-
OKEMAH. Okla

Though they ran no photographs, the Oklahoma newspapers did cover the event. Its genesis could be traced to an incident several weeks previous, when a sheriff's posse searched the cabin of a black family named Nelson, living in Okemah. Several cows were missing from a nearby ranch, and the posse was looking for stolen meat. During the search Nelson's son, a teenager, shot and killed a deputy. Laura Nelson, knowing how the deed would be received, claimed to have shot the man in order to protect her son. But her innocence was common knowledge. Nelson's father pled guilty to stealing cattle "and was taken to the pen, which probably saved his life."

A few weeks later, the jailer at Okemah was surprised in the night by a mob of forty men, who demanded to see the Nelsons. With a gun held to his head, the guard unlocked the cell where the son was sleeping. The mob rousted him out, "fourteen and yellow and ignorant," according to the papers, and then "stifled and gagged" him. "Next they went up to the female jail (a cage in the courthouse) and took the woman out." She was "very small of stature, very black, about thirty-five years old," the newspapers reported, "and vicious." Mother and son were taken to the steel bridge, located "in a negro settlement," and hanged. "The woman's arms were swinging at her side, untied, while about twenty feet away swung the boy with his clothes partly torn off and his hands tied with a saddle string…Gently swaying in the wind, the ghastly spectacle was discovered by a Negro boy taking his cow to water. Hundreds of people from Okemah and the western part of the country went to view the scene."[3] One newspaper also remarked, "While the general sentiment is adverse to the method, it is generally thought that the Negroes got what would have been due them under process of law"—though it is not clear which part of the Oklahoma penal code made lying to protect one's son a capital offense.

"No attempt to follow the mob was made," noted the papers. Afterward the district judge convened a grand jury to investigate. No one in the community was able or willing to identify any of the forty men responsible. This left the judge distinctly unhappy:

> The people of the state have said by recently adopted constitutional provision that the race to which the unfortunate victims belonged should in large measure be divorced from participation in our political contests, because of their known racial inferiority and their dependent credulity, which very characteristic made them the mere tool of the designing and cunning. It is well known that I heartily concur in this constitutional provision of the people's will. The more then does the duty devolve upon us of a superior race and of greater intelligence to protect this weaker race from unjustifiable and lawless attacks.

The photograph taken May 25 was copyrighted by G. H. Farnum and copies were sold as postcards, as was a close-up of Laura Nelson that Farnum also took from his boat. Such cards were not uncommon, for the simple reason that lynchings were not uncommon at the turn of the century, especially in the South. Between 1880 and 1930 at least thirty-three hundred African Americans were murdered by mobs. During the 1890s and early 1900s, two or three blacks on average were hanged, burned, or otherwise killed every week. Nobody much minded seeing or being seen. An observer at a lynching in Fayette County, Tennessee, in 1915 noted, "Hundreds of kodaks clicked all morning at the scene of the lynching…Picture card photographers installed a portable printing plant at the bridge and reaped a harvest in selling postcards…At a number of country schools the day's routine was delayed until boy and girl pupils could get back from viewing the lynched man."[4]

Some white Southerners found the practice barbarous. "If our grand jury won't indict these lynchers, if our petit juries won't convict, and if our soldiers won't shoot, what are we coming to?" asked the mayor of Statesboro, Georgia. But other high officials were not so shocked. "I led the mob which lynched Nelse Patton, and I am proud of it," declared a former United States senator from Mississippi in 1908. Three years later, when a mob dismembered a black man at Honea Path, South Carolina, that state's governor declared he would have "come to Honea Path and led the mob," if his services had been needed "in punishing that nigger brute."[5]

Brute. Those who did the lynching were certain that the white race had justice on its side. As long as blacks cast their "lustful eyes on white women," announced the *Little Rock Daily News,* "as long as any of them seek to break down the barrier that has been between the Negro and white man for a thousand years," then Southern whites would not be "slow or timid" to punish. "This may be 'Southern brutality' as far as the Boston Negro can see, but in polite circles, we call it Southern chivalry." The *Memphis Commercial* made a similar point in 1892. "The generation of Negroes which have grown up since the [Civil] war," it warned, "have lost in large measure the traditional and wholesome awe of the white race which kept the Negroes in subjection…There is no longer a restraint upon the brute passion of the Negro."[6]

The woman who brought that statement to the attention of a national audience, and held it up to withering scorn, was a passionate young woman by the name of Ida B. Wells. Like Laura Nelson, Wells was small of stature and relatively dark of complexion. No doubt she too was considered "vicious" by newspapers like the *Daily Commercial*. The great majority of lynching victims were male, but if a black woman spoke out too boldly she too might find herself the target of racial rage. Wells discovered this firsthand. After some of the city's angry whites read her denunciation of lynching, they threatened very publicly, she reported, to have her "hanged in front of the court-house and my face bled."[7]

She had not started out as a rabble-rouser. A decade earlier Ida B. Wells had arrived in Memphis as a proper young schoolteacher ready to further her education at the local teacher's college and enjoy a night out at the theater. She was eager to sample the multitude of fashionable wares offered by department stores like Menken's Palatial Emporium. She longed to worship at the city's many churches, black and white. She came of age as one of that first generation of African Americans in the years following emancipation. In that sense the first three decades of her life reflected the uncertain and uncharted path many were following, to discover what it meant to be a free black woman in Victorian America.

This is the story of Wells's first thirty years. It is not a biography strictly speaking, for other good ones exist. It is not a history of lynching—that subject too has received much scholarly attention. Rather, it is an attempt to chart one woman's steps toward personal and cultural self-definition—steps that were thwarted by a movement to hedge in African Americans according to the evolving racial constructs of the day. Reconstruction in the political sense, under which the South was brought back into the Union, ended in 1877. But the reconstruction of *race* as a concept and as a social and political weapon continued through the final decades of the century and beyond. Like so many other black Americans, Wells found that she could forge her own identity only by challenging and contesting the second-class citizenship that emerged out of that reconstruction of race.

The act of lynching, she discovered in 1892, was at the center of that reconstruction. "Eight negroes lynched," she wrote angrily:

> ... one at Little Rock, Ark., last Saturday Morning where the citizens broke into the penitentiary and got their man; three near Anniston, Ala., one near New Orleans; and three at Clarksville, Ga., the last three for killing a white man, and five on the same old racket—the new alarm about raping white women. The same programme of hanging, then shooting bullets into the lifeless bodies was carried out to the letter.
>
> Nobody in this section of the country believes the old thread bare lie that Negro men rape white women. If Southern white men are not careful, they will over-reach themselves and public sentiment will have a reaction.[8]

Meantime, she decided she had better be ready. She bought a pistol. "I felt that one had better die fighting against injustice than to die like a dog or a rat in a trap."[9]

And Wells kept on writing. It was a matter, after all, of self-definition. "If I am not who you say I am," wrote a later African American still struggling with what it meant to be black, "then you are not who you think you are."

· *One* ·

Into a Changing World

❦

T HE WOMAN WHO EAGERLY AWAITED THE CHANCE TO BE photographed—who thought the camera could "catch" her likeness—instinctively distinguished between her true identity and what the camera might or might not catch. The world observes us and, inevitably, makes rough and ready judgments about our character based on a host of categories that come with their own expectations: married/unmarried; immigrant/native born; Christian/Jew. Some categories we accept as a reasonable reflection of who we are. Others strike us as misleading and provoke us to push back. But they are applied and used, just as we apply and use them on others—and on ourselves. *They say/we say . . .*

Ida Wells was born in the town of Holly Springs, Mississippi, on July 16, 1862, during a civil war in which one of the most basic categories humans have used to define one another—*slave* versus *free*—was being eliminated in the United States. Ida's mother, Elizabeth Wells, was a cook whose culinary reputation had spread through Holly Springs. Her father, James, was a carpenter, also respected. Both were slaves. Three days before Lizzie Wells took to bed to deliver her daughter, Abraham Lincoln confided to members of his cabinet that he intended to issue a declaration setting in motion the end of slavery. Lincoln announced the Emancipation Proclamation in September, when Ida was two months old, indicating that it would go into effect on January 1, 1863.

What did the proclamation mean to the Wells family? Or for that matter, to the fifteen thousand enslaved African Americans living in Marshall County around Holly Springs?[1] Everything and nothing. Technically, Lincoln's declaration freed not a single slave—in Marshall County or anywhere else. It applied only to those slaves living behind Confederate lines, where the Union had no power to enforce its decree. And in September 1862 Confederate territory included Holly Springs, nine hundred miles southwest of Washington in northern Mississippi.

Then, a little more than a month before the proclamation went into effect, General Ulysses S. Grant began moving Union troops out of Tennessee south along the rail lines running from Memphis and Grand Junction. Those lines crossed at Holly Springs. Grant had his eye on Vicksburg, farther south, but in setting up his advance he transformed Holly Springs into a depot for Union supplies—filling the public buildings, the Masonic temple, and even churches with food, equipment, and ammunition. To a town of no more than four thousand, witnessing some forty-five thousand troops passing through, it must have seemed as though half of Yankeedom had come to stay.[2]

Except that most of the soldiers kept moving south. And as dawn broke on December 20, Confederate general Earl Van Dorn rode down on Holly Springs with twenty-five hundred cavalry. Delighted white residents struggled out into the chill morning to cheer (many women still in their nightclothes, "disheveled hair floating in the winter wind"),[3] as the rebels set fire to Union storehouses, scattering

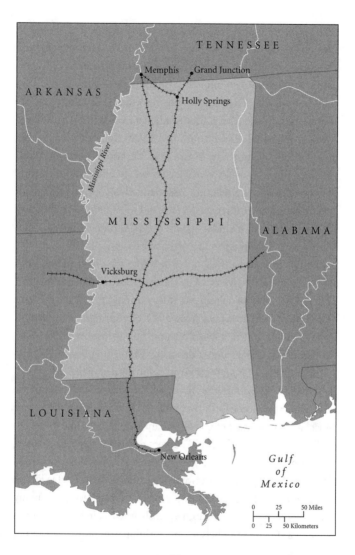

the sentries left in town. Van Dorn retreated by four in the afternoon, but the raid was a taste of things to come. During the war, Holly Springs changed hands at least fifty-nine times.[4]

In a countryside where no one knew from one month to the next who controlled which towns, plantations, and roads, what could the Emancipation Proclamation mean? In Holly Springs, as in countless locales all across the South, freedom was not being defined by words from Washington. It was being defined on the ground, individual by individual. Enslaved African Americans had to decide for themselves whether to break for freedom, and the decision was never easy.

Yet if, in the fog of battle, the proclamation seemed to mean nothing, in other ways it meant everything. For it demonstrated that the conflict between North and South had become more than a war to reunite whites—the war for Union that Lincoln first proclaimed. (Blacks were not and could not become American citizens, insisted the Supreme Court in the *Dred Scott* decision of 1857, because the black man had no rights "which the white man is bound to respect.") For slaves trying to gauge the war's effect on their own situation, the Emancipation Proclamation provided a new light—a light many had been eagerly anticipating for months and even years—as their masters knew.

It was impossible to keep the news of John Brown's attack on Harper's Ferry from spreading. We slaves knew very little about what was going on outside our plantations, for our owners aimed to keep us in darkness. But sometimes, by grapevine telegraph, we learned of great events. (George Albright, Marshall County)

Every political speech…attracted a number of negroes, who, without entering the Hall, have managed to linger around and hear what the orators say. (A Georgia newspaper editor)

The first knowledge that I got of the fact that we were slaves, and that freedom of the slaves was being discussed, was early one morning before day, when I was awakened by my mother kneeling over her children and fervently praying that Lincoln and his armies might be successful, and that one day she and her children might be free. (Booker T. Washington, Virginia)[5]

Grant discovered this hunger for freedom in the fall of 1862 during his march toward Holly Springs. As Confederate planters fled before the Union army, slaves flocked behind the lines in "vast numbers" that astonished the troops. Around Grand Junction, Tennessee, reported one officer, crowds turned out "garbed in rags or in silks, with feet shod or bleeding, individually or in families and larger groups—an army of slaves and fugitives" whose arrival "was like the oncoming of cities."[6] When Van Dorn's raids forced the Union army back into Tennessee for a time, slaves who had collected around Holly Springs were determined not to return to their former lives. They jammed every available space on a train of freight and passenger cars and when those spaces were filled, they clambered atop the roofs, freezing as the cars lumbered along the wintry, fifty-mile ride to Memphis.[7]

Living in Holly Springs, Jim and Lizzie Wells witnessed this ingathering and exodus. Both worked for Spires Bolling, a prosperous builder who had designed the elegant house where Ida was born,[8] only blocks from the center of town. With Ida only six months old, her parents hesitated to flee in a time of chaos. By war's end the birth of sister Eugenia only made flight more daunting. Confederate deserters continually harassed the countryside, making the trip uncertain, though that did not stop thousands of former slaves even after the war was over.[9] In any case, Jim Wells

The home of Spires Bolling, now the Ida B. Wells-Barnett Museum

recognized that Holly Springs, devastated by raids and counter-raids, would need good carpenters to rebuild. Spires Bolling himself was eager to employ him—henceforth as a free man.

But what would freedom mean in practice? First reactions could be both intoxicating and bewildering, for at times it seemed the world had turned upside down. "White man is nigger and nigger is white man," declared one defeated Confederate, while in conquered Richmond, jubilant black soldiers took turns swiveling in the Speaker's chair, where the Confederate Congress had convened.[10] Jim and Lizzie Wells were not given to such extreme sentiments; they didn't intend to uproot their lives to start anew. Yet they were determined life would not go on as before—neither for them nor for their daughters. Lizzie knew firsthand how slavery destroyed families. She had grown up in Virginia as one of nine siblings, been beaten harshly on more than one occasion, then sold off and taken over the mountains to Mississippi's rich cotton lands. She never saw her parents again. Once free she tried to trace her family in Virginia, without success.

Jim Wells didn't have to search for his family. He had been born only a few dozen miles from Holly Springs in Tippah County, though under more ambiguous circumstances. His mother Peggy was a slave, but his father was white and master of the plantation. This master never had children by his white wife, "Miss Polly." No doubt partly for that reason, he treated his mulatto son kindly. Jim was "the companion and comfort" of his father, Ida recalled years later.[11] He would not be sent to hard labor in the fields. When Jim turned eighteen, his father and master took him to Holly Springs and apprenticed him to learn carpentry under Spires Bolling.[12]

Slavery destroyed families, warped relationships. One of the first ways in which Jim and Lizzie expressed their freedom was to formalize their marriage, as did many freed folk after the war. Sometimes they married in couples, as Jim and Lizzie did, sometimes in group ceremonies that included well over one hundred people.[13] But marriage was only one custom among many distorted by bondage. Even the simplest acts had to be rethought with the coming of freedom. Before the war, when Jim Wells proceeded along the sidewalks of Holly Springs, a prescribed range of behaviors was expected of him. If he walked with Spires Bolling, he knew to follow respectfully a pace or two to the rear. If he were alone and a white neighbor approached, he had to tip his hat and speak only when spoken to. If spoken to, he had to address the neighbor by his title and last name, "Mr. Johnson, sir." He had to take care to be humble. And he had to yield the sidewalk if there were not ample space for the two to pass. A white passerby, on the other hand, never doffed his hat, never yielded the sidewalk, and was free to ignore Wells entirely or to ask any question he pleased.

After the war, walking down the street became an act of conscious calculation. Many African Americans determined to set a new tone and whites were astonished—even slack-jawed—at the change:

> During my walks from one shop to another I sometimes had to get off the side walk into the street in order to make way for these [blue uniformed] negro soldiers—they walked four and five abreast and made not the slightest effort to let white women pass. (A lady in Memphis)
>
> It is the first time in my life that I have ever had to give up the sidewalk to a man, much less to negroes! (A Georgia woman)
>
> It is impossible to describe the condition of the city—It is so unlike anything we could imagine—Negroes shoving white persons off the walk. (A planter in Charleston)[14]

Were they actually "shoving"? *They say.* It was not always easy to be sure. Had the whites on the sidewalk tried to push the black pedestrians off first, as was their "right"? Northern observers noted that the feelings of defeated Southerners were often set to a hair trigger. "They perceive insolence in a tone, a glance, a gesture, or failure to yield enough by two or three inches in meeting on the sidewalk," commented one traveler. "Southern whites are quite indignant if they are not treated with the same deference that they were accustomed to," remarked another, while a Virginian acknowledged to a reporter from the *Nation* that some of his countrymen "can't see a nigger go along the street now-a-days that they don't damn him for putting on airs."[15]

Insolence; putting on airs: these qualities were perceived not only in the failure to yield the sidewalk but in such basic matters as names. As young Ida grew old enough to walk around Holly Springs on her own, how would white folk address her? Under slavery, whites were used to addressing blacks by just about any familiar name they chose: boy, uncle, auntie . "Last week, in Chattanooga, I said to a nigger I found at the railroad, 'Here, Buck! Show me the baggage-room,'" reported one white man after the war. "He said, 'My name a'n't Buck.' I just put my six-shooter to his head, and by—! He didn't stop to think what his name was, but showed me what I wanted." A young white woman in her teens would be addressed as "Miss," but for Ida to insist upon such niceties risked causing a scene. "What you doin', nigger?" called an Alabama master to his young slave. "I ain't no nigger, I'se a Negro and I'm Miss Liza Mixon," she replied. The master grabbed a switch and chased her until she was caught and whipped.[16]

Yet the acts of walking downtown or greeting a neighbor involved only the most elementary of behaviors. In April 1866 Congress reversed the *Dred Scott* decision by passing the Civil Rights Act, and in doing so began the process toward extending citizenship to African Americans. The act gave them the right to own property, make contracts, and participate in the court system. The Fourteenth Amendment, ratified by June 1868, put the guarantee of citizenship into the Constitution and added the promise of due process of law. How would Jim Wells exercise those rights day to day, nine hundred miles from Washington? Where would Lizzie Wells or her children go to school if they wanted the education forbidden them under slavery? If white and black expectations were at odds even over sidewalks, how difficult would it be for Ida and her parents to define freedom differently in a host of other ways?

❦

For Jim Wells, one way to define freedom and shape it was by participating in politics. Growing up, Ida took her first impressions of civic life from the actions of her father. She remembered him as a god-fearing man, as generous with his feelings as he was with his time.[17] He valued civic duty and was a joiner: a member of the Masons and also on the board of trustees for Shaw University, one of the new schools for blacks in Holly Springs. He didn't run for political office, but he understood that having the vote was essential to possessing freedom. He took a keen interest politics and followed the news in the papers. Sometimes he would get Ida to read the news aloud, an accomplishment that made him intensely proud.

The political meetings had started during the war, with something called the "4-Ls:" Lincoln's Legal Loyal League. The League had been organized by Northerners who filtered into Holly Springs. It later came to be called the Loyal League or Union League. In addition to the Holly Springs chapter, there were branches in Byhalia, Red Banks, Tallaloosa, Chulahoma, and all over the state—all over the South, for that matter. Secrecy was paramount, with members attending late-night meetings and using passwords, special knocks, and signs.[18]

After the war there was less need for stealth, at least in Holly Springs, where a federal garrison housed more than a hundred soldiers.[19] With federals around, the League felt free to meet in the black Baptist church or at the home of Captain Nelson G. Gill, a white Union veteran from Illinois who was chapter president. Given Jim Wells's interest in politics, he almost certainly became a member, initiated in a solemn ceremony. Standing in a circle before an altar decorated with a ballot box, flag or similar emblems, new members clasped hands, lifting them high, as the room was darkened and a fire of liberty kindled. Then each member swore "upon the Holy Bible, Declaration of Independence, and the Constitution of the United States of America" to "defend this State against any invasion, insurrection or rebellion" and "elect true and reliable Union men and supporters of the government."

To help members understand the purposes of the organization, the League furnished a dialogue between "a white Republican and a colored citizen," which Gill and another member could read aloud. In some League chapters "the whole house would ring with shouts" when the answers were given, especially to the more pointed questions.[20]

Q. Who freed the slaves of the South?
A. Abraham Lincoln, the Republican President, by proclamation.
Q. Who passed the Freedman's Bureau Bill?
A. A Republican Congress by more than a two-thirds vote over the veto of Andrew Johnson, the leader of the Democratic or conservative party.
Q. Who gave us the Civil Rights Bill?
A. The same Republican Congress.
Q. What party gave us the right to vote?
A. The Republican party.
Q. With whom do the disloyal white men of the South desire the colored men to vote?

A. With the Democratic party.

Q. Would not the Democrats take away all the negro's rights?

A. They would.

Q. Then why do they pretend to be the best friends of the colored men?[21]

Old Judge Watson in town was one of those "friendly" Democrats: someone who had opposed secession but then joined the Confederacy, since he couldn't bring himself to "go against his blood and kindred." When the white legislature tried to bring back virtual slavery after the war, in the form of a "black code" restricting African American freedoms, the judge thought the code was going "entirely too far." He and others wanted to achieve a "good understanding between the white and colored men."[22]

During election season in Marshall County, white Democrats would sometimes hold a barbecue and invite the freedmen. Many who came promised to vote Democratic, but didn't; they came mostly for the food. Others arrived to taunt their foes, sporting oilcloth caps and red feathers, badges of the Republican Party. They'd been bossed or harassed too long to believe any talk of cooperation. In any case most Mississippi whites scorned folk like Judge Watson for "making negro speeches, getting up negro meetings, and playing second fiddle to Sambo."[23]

Jim Wells was never tempted to desert the Republicans. His first chance to vote came in the fall of 1867, when delegates were elected to write a new state constitution. Spires Bolling made his opinion known that Wells should vote Democratic. On election day, citizens cast ballots on tickets printed by the rival parties. Each party ticket had its own distinctive look. As voters deposited their ballots, election judges could usually tell how people

"The First Vote," Harper's Weekly, November 16, 1867

voted. Wells was not deterred. He went with the Republican ticket and news of his choice traveled fast. When he returned home, he found himself locked out of his tool shop. Old man Bolling had made his feelings known.

Wells made his feelings known too. Directly, he walked downtown and bought a new set of tools, had his family collect their belongings, and moved them out of the house on Randolph Avenue—all before Bolling returned home. Another man might have thought it best to pile everything in a cart and leave town. Wells merely "went across the street," Ida recalled, "and rented another house," right under Bolling's nose.[24]

The Union League meant to go head to head with the Democrats. Republicans had the votes to command, for nearly 60 percent of Marshall County was black. Gill, the Union veteran who ran the League in Holly Springs, drilled members to march. Some days, black members of the League would take the day off to attend militia meetings. During election seasons, folk from all around the county poured into Holly Springs, forming a parade line that stretched a mile some days. League members wore red sashes and large red and blue badges. Gill led the procession, his "red sash flying in the wind," horns and drums making a fanfare. Whites in town closed up their houses, but enough peered from their windows to report that a float passed made up of a cart with a tree in it, several possums hiding in the branches, and a "huge negro" standing by. The Negro was singing "loudly as he could…'Carve that 'possum, nigger, carve him to the heart.'" It chilled the blood of some watching to see those white possums treed by such a bold black man.[25]

More thrilling for League marchers—and more frightening for whites—were the torchlight parades. Jim Wells would go to a march like that! Before the war, whites owned the night and had formed patrols that chased any slave who went hunting or tried to sneak a visit to a family member at a neighboring plantation. Now hundreds, even thousands of blacks filled the town streets campaigning, as whites had done since the beginning of the republic. Along they marched with torches and "transparencies"—pictures painted on thin cloth, ten to twelve feet long—the entire scene lit in an eerie, flickering glow. The banners were covered with "obscene pictures," reported two leading ladies of Holly Springs, "particularly of the Democratic candidates." The Democrats, of course, had their own torches and transparencies. To them it seemed hardly obscene—only a matter of "great pomp and ceremony"—to carry a coffin, in a mock funeral procession for Captain Gill.

Gill stood up to all manner of provocation without losing his temper. Once when he was making a speech in the state legislature, Colonel Street "walked up to him, pulled his beard and shook him." The captain "submitted as tamely as possible, no resentment of this insult being at all apparent in his face, manner, or conduct." Such conduct was beyond all comprehension to a true Southerner, who would have felt obliged to take "the satisfaction of a gentleman" by whipping anyone challenging his honor.[26]

In only a few years the government of Marshall County had been transformed. By the time Ida was six or seven years old, big enough to walk to the center of town with her mother, she would have spied the building on the southeast corner of the town square occupied by blue-coated soldiers. This was the office of the Bureau of Refugees, Freedmen, and Abandoned Lands—popularly known as Freedmen's Bureau. Its head, Captain Sturgis, prosecuted cases brought before him against whites as well as blacks, as part of the Freedman's Bureau's mission to help newly freed slaves. Governor Adelbert Ames, a Republican, began appointing loyal Republican officials in 1869, though the first time blacks voted in a normal Mississippi election was 1871. By 1874, when Ida was twelve years old and very much aware of the political currents swirling through the town, the Board of Supervisors included Gill, along with three black members and a single conservative white. The new leadership increased the funds to aid paupers and established a poorhouse. New bridges were built as well as new schoolhouses.[27]

Most whites resented the changes. Too much was being spent on schools, they said, too much on the rug for the new courthouse. Beyond specific complaints, what rankled most seemed to be the boldness of the new politics. Whites resented it when Captain Sturgis of the Freedman's Bureau "made himself very obnoxious to the people by arresting and dragging before his tribunal persons for miles around on the mere accusation of a negro."[28] Beginning in 1866 in Pulaski, Tennessee, some whites began to organize themselves as the Ku Klux Klan, to take a more active role in suppressing such "obnoxious" behavior on the part of blacks.[29]

Ida first encountered the strange words—*Ku Klux Klan*—in the newspaper or heard them whispered by her parents. As a young girl she had no idea what the phrase meant, only that the Klan was "something fearful." Her mother especially was determined that their home should be a refuge, where their children might be brought up safely and respectably. "So far as I can remember there were no riots in Holly Springs," Ida recalled. Yet when her father went to his evening meetings, Lizzie stayed up, pacing the floor, until he had returned home safe.[30]

In Marshall County the "regulation disguise" of the "Klu Kluxers" (as some called them) was said to be "black and red entirely," though other freedmen remembered "Injun rubber clothes" and "white gowns with something black in front and a great big tin button that looked like an owl at night."[31] Klan initiations included a solemn oath, nearly the opposite in import from the Union League's. "You do solemnly swear, in the presence of Almighty God and before this assembly of witnesses, that you will do the acts commanded of you by the commander of this Ku Klux Klan, outside of the civil law, so help you God." There were questions and answers too:

Q. What are the objects of the Ku Klux Klan?
A. It is to suppress the negro and keep him in the position where he belongs, and to see that the Democratic party controls this country.[32]

In Marshall County, the Klan had perhaps fifteen to twenty "dens." Henry C. Myers, promoted to the rank of Cyclops and "a man of splendid family," played a key role in organizing.[33] Klan members began almost immediately to undercut the "civil law" of the county, not least the Freedman's Bureau courts, overseen by Captain Sturgis. "In more than one case [Sturgis] had white women brought before him, and this proceeding so angered the Democratic white men that they paid him a visit. Five prominent young men of the community, members of the Ku Klux Klan, dressed in the full regalia of the klan, went to his office one night, and warned him that the bringing of white women before the bureau must be stopped, or the klan would punish him accordingly. This warning was sufficient; for the women of the county were not molested again."[34]

There were larger goals too, one of which was to disarm blacks throughout the county. On a single night, the various dens rode from plantation to plantation, stopping in every black home they could reach and demanding all firearms.[35] Although Ida remembered no "riots" in the county, there was the occasional "little battle," as Marshall's white historian put it. At one Holly Springs rally, where some three or four thousand blacks gathered, Nelson Gill was attacked by Colonel Myers, the Klan Cyclops, who jumped onto the platform as the rest of the white mob pelted the speakers with sticks and brickbats, breaking the leg of one of the Republican candidates.[36]

Because Gill was constantly at the head of parades, "exhorting his 'black army' onward,"[37] he became a Klan target. Several members of the organization hid one night under Gill's house, where they took a bead on the captain during a League meeting. Just as the assassin pulled the trigger, the Klansman next to him (reviled by some as being entirely too "tender-hearted") deflected the pistol, sending the shot wild and forcing the attackers to flee. From then on, Union Leaguers posted sentries; no doubt Lizzie's worries for her husband increased.[38]

On election day, black voters rode to the polls four abreast on horseback, making a ceremony of the occasion. If they lacked a horse or donkey, they borrowed one after someone else had

Voters at a Louisiana parish

voted. Large groups meant safety. Better to vote at the town square in Holly Springs rather than in some out-of-the-way place, where whites could threaten more easily. At one of the gates to the courtyard in Holly Springs, Gill would set up a carpetbag full of tickets on top of a little crate, then hand them out and pass folks through in groups of ten. The ballots were also distributed the day before by Union League members, making the rounds of local voters.[39]

Republican successes only made the Democrats and the Klan push harder. Registration period, when citizens could enroll to vote, was always difficult. There were three registrars empowered to qualify voters, who went from town to town together. In 1871, the Democratic official was Henry Myers, the Klan Cyclops, who "refused to qualify any young negro unless he brought reliable evidence as to his age." How many freedmen could produce a birth certificate or witnesses whom Myers would accept? When Ben Phillips, the black registrar, objected to Myers' challenges "in an insolent manner," Myers picked up the nearest chair and swung at Phillips's head.[40]

As election day approached, ballot tickets had to be printed. Gill wanted something distinctive, to help voters who couldn't read. He sent a colleague, J. L. Burton, to a printer in Memphis to place the order. Burton, however, discovered that he was being followed by a private detective hired by the Democrats. Burton put in an order in Memphis that was only a decoy, then headed several hundred miles up river for St. Louis, to place his real order. The dogged detective followed and discovered that the Republican tickets were bright red; he then rushed back to report, in time for the Democrats to use red as well.

Burton had one last feint. Tickets in hand, he went to a different printing shop after the detective departed and ordered a black tiger printed on each. Around Marshall County, word went out to Republicans to use the tickets with the tiger.

Democrats discovered the change only the night before the election. In haste they approached the wife of the party chairman in Holly Springs, an amateur artist. Working late, the woman carved a tiger on a wood block, which was then stamped onto the Democratic tickets. The only difference was that "the tiger ran up the Democratic tickets, while he ran down the Republicans." Since most voters folded their ballots when placing them in the box, the images didn't show. By nine o'clock election-day morning, the Democrats had managed to spread their tickets throughout the county. Many voters were under the mistaken impression that they were voting Republican.

A few white Mississipians still believed cooperation was the most prudent course. But most moderates found it hard to bear up under white threats and the stony silence of their neighbors. As the election of 1875 approached, Judge Watson and several moderate white ministers went to Klansman Henry Myers. Hat in hand, the judge asked Myers if he couldn't run a fair election this time around. Myers knew the black population of the county as well as the judge. They would have to "resort to fraud or else continue under negro domination," Myers replied.

Watson hesitated. He didn't like either alternative.

"Well," he said at last, "we shan't have any more negro rule."[41]

Jim Wells couldn't miss the same message. The newspapers had begun to talk about drawing a "white line" that kept blacks out of government. They even emblazoned it on the mastheads of their papers. "Mississippi is a white man's country, and by the Eternal God we'll rule it." This proclamation came from Yazoo county.

In the summer of 1874, the papers reported riots with increasing frequency. A Negro girl was shot in Austin, and the sheriff let her killer go. When blacks met to protest, whites shot six of the crowd. In Vicksburg, whites overthrew the black city government, and some thirty blacks who turned out to protest were mowed down by gunfire. Another dozen near Macon were killed by whites on horseback. The message was clear: hold a political meeting at the risk of your life.

Now the bands of armed men didn't even bother with hooded masks or the darkness of night; they broke up meetings in broad daylight. As election day approached, desperate freedmen across the state wrote Governor Ames. "I beg you most fulley to send the United soldiers here," said one. "They have hung six more men since the killing of Mr. Fawn; they wont let the republican have no ticket." Another protested, "Dear sir, did not the 14th Article [of the Constitution] ... say that no person shall be deprived of life nor property without due process of law? It said all persons have equal protection of the laws but I say we colored men don't get it at all ... Is that right, or is it not? No, sir, it is wrong."[42]

In Holly Springs, Gill did his best to rally Republicans. He was running for sheriff, the most powerful office in the county. On election day, the captain came to the town square and set up his stand. The Republican ballots this time were a reddish purple, an American flag on the back. They were easy to distinguish from the Democratic ticket, which was lily white—there was no missing where that "white line" was drawn.

No matter. At the opposite end of the square sat Booker Aston and John Price. They were "Democratic Negroes"—they'd always seen where their bread was buttered and "went with their white folks."[43] Henry Myers, the Klansman, had placed them there. Gill got voters, of course, but plenty of black men took white tickets from Aston and Price. Some voters didn't even fold them, to show more clearly who they were voting for. When the votes were counted, the Democrats had won by a considerable majority. Gill was defeated for sheriff. The winner, who took charge of law enforcement throughout the county, was the Klansman Henry Myers.

Coming home from the polls, Jim Wells was sorely discouraged. Across the South, the former Confederate states were being "redeemed," their governments wrenched back onto the other side of that white line. In the presidential election of 1876 the results were even worse. Reconstruction had ended. Republicans in the North largely abandoned Southern blacks to the fates determined by the new white "redeemer" governments. And although the legal distinction of *slave* versus *free* had been abolished, the white line based on the notion of race shone brighter than ever.

Jim Wells and thousands of other black men had sought to define themselves as free men through the power of the ballot box—in vain. Ida Wells, who turned fourteen only months before the election of 1876, witnessed her father's frustrations as that avenue of self-definition was blocked. She would have to seek a different path to enlarge her freedom.

· *Two* ·

A MORAL EDUCATION

❦

ABOUT THE TIME THAT MARSHALL COUNTY DEMOCRATS "redeemed" its government and whites across the South ended Reconstruction, Ida enrolled at Shaw University in Holly Springs. Her schooling, though, began at such an early age, she couldn't remember learning to read.[1]

The urge to learn was not surprising. The coming of emancipation brought with it a fierce desire on the part of freedpeople to master what had long been forbidden. By law, a slave caught reading in Mississippi before the war was liable to receive thirty-nine lashes; widespread rumor had it that a thumb could be cut off too ("above the second joint," recalled George Albright of Holly Springs). No matter. Deep in the woods slaves would dig pits, cover them with vines, then "slip out of the Quarters at night" where "some nigger that had some learning would have a school."[2] Or a slave might filch a copy of Noah Webster's dictionary, "the blue-back speller," as a guide; or listen through a window to a plantation tutor giving lessons.[3] Belle Caruthers, near Holly Springs, took advantage of being a wet nurse in her master's home. "The baby had Alphabet Blocks to play with and I learned my letters while she learned hers. There was a Blue Back Speller there too and one day the master caught me studying it, and he struck me with his muddy boot." She wasn't discouraged. "I found a hymn book one day and spelled out, 'When I Can Read My Title Clear.' I was so happy when I saw that I could really read, that I ran around telling all the other slaves. After the war I went to Gill's school in Holly Springs."[4]

Nelson Gill and his wife tended the school in town allied with the Baptists. The other school, run by the Methodists, was Shaw University. Both were staffed by Northern missionaries, along with at least one literate African American, and offered instruction beginning with elementary school and moving upward. (In those days many schools styled themselves colleges and universities regardless of the level of their curriculum.) Enthusiasm for education ran high, even during the war. In Arkansas, one traveler encountered within a fairly small region, "Uncle Jack, a colored man, at the Goodrich place...teaching a school of eighty-nine scholars" as well as "a school taught by Rose Anna, a colored girl," at the Groshon plantation. Not far away, William McCutcheon presided over sixty students using "books of every kind and description," while Uncle Tom, at the Savage plantation, helped about thirty students, even though "he is infirm, and teaches them remaining himself in bed."[5] East of Holly Springs students could be found "every hour of daylight at their books," a chaplain reported. "We cannot enter a cabin or tent, but that we see from one to three with books." Once Reconstruction was under way, "there was a schoolhouse every four or five miles" in Marshall County, "wherever there was a thick settlement."[6]

Ida Wells joined this flood of students under the determined direction of her parents. Lizzie went to school along with her children, as so many older freedpeople did. She was especially determined to read the Bible. She was "awake," like so many former slaves, "to the possibility of *their children* becoming 'something,'" as one missionary teacher put it.[7]

Then too, whites in Holly Springs were proud of the town's educational opportunities for both young men and women. Before the war, eleven academies had operated at one time or another, including the University of Holly Springs, St. Thomas Hall, Franklin Female College, and the Holly Springs Female Institute. African Americans in town could see for themselves how much education was valued.

Knowledge was not only power, it was a path to a world of culture and polish long monopolized by the planters and middle-class whites. It was a way to rise above the backbreaking work of the fields and sleeping on "one-legged Aggie" beds nailed to the wall in the corner of a poor log cabin.[8] Lizzie and Jim would have known about productions of the Holly Springs Dramatic Association, which performed in the second-story auditorium of the Opera House. The stage boasted a curtain and thirteen sets of scenery.[9]

At least a few whites in town favored instruction for African Americans. "However hostile to the education of the Freedmen the whites may be elsewhere in the South, here both teachers and pupils are respected and encouraged by the most influential of them," noted Shaw University's annual report in 1875.[10] Not everyone approved. In nearby Memphis when whites looted African American neighborhoods after the war, they singled out a dozen black schools for destruction.[11] In Holly Springs, hostility showed

A schoolhouse burns in Memphis riots, 1866

itself on the sidewalks of the town square. Gill's school let out about the same time each afternoon as the Female Institute and Bethlehem Academy; the students from each flocked home in groups. The whites, of course, claimed right of way, but Mrs. Gill would no more cede that territory than her husband would back off in politics. She placed herself "in the center of her black column, and her pupils would lock arms so as to form a solid wall across the sidewalk. The white girls would have to pass around, or"—dreaded alternative—"come into contact with the negroes."[12]

Though Ida's love of learning mirrored that of other freed-people, she stood well above the majority in talent and ambition. She read every book in the Sunday school library, scanned newspapers, read all the plays of Shakespeare, and worked through the Bible from Genesis to the Revelation to John. Lizzie encouraged this religious study by forbidding her children to read any volume but the Bible on the Sabbath.

With books in short supply, freedman's schools used what came to hand, from Clark's *First Lessons in English Grammar* to the poems of Alfred Lord Tennyson or texts produced for such schools, like *The Freedman's Book*. Ida would have joined in the rote question-and-answer sessions similar in style to those of the Union League. No doubt she sang "John Brown's Body" too, the unofficial version of Julia Ward Howe's "Battle Hymn of the Republic." That song raised eyebrows in more than one Southern town when the voices of young freedmen loudly mocked the Confederacy's ex-president with the verse, "They shall hang Jeff Davis to a sour apple tree."[13]

Because the Wellses were Methodist, Ida attended Shaw, where Jim Wells was a member of the board of trustees. Compulsory chapel was held every day and prayer meetings every week, not to mention church on Sundays. And although religion infused

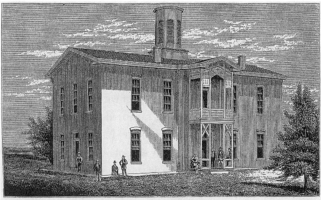

SHAW UNIVERSITY, HOLLY SPRINGS, MISS.

Shaw University (later renamed Rust College), in 1878

Ida's education, Shaw's curriculum was also hard-nosed. Albert McDonald, the mechanic and preacher who helped Nelson Gill organize the local Union League, was one of Shaw's founders. The school did not pretend to be a full-blown college, he explained, "seeking to hurry students through a college curriculum…sending them into the battle of life only to disgrace themselves and bring reproach upon the cause of education at large, but to take the far more difficult and tedious plan of trying to lay well a foundation for a broad, thorough and practical education."[14] Ida confessed later that she received little preparation in algebra or the sciences, but in grammar, language, and literature, Shaw did well by its students.[15] Ida wrote with a careful hand: "large, well-formed letters…words written precisely on each line and slanted slightly to the right."[16] Her extensive vocabulary reflected a familiarity with the Bible, writing of "the cool of the evening" or of "hewers and drawers." Her Shakespeare stuck too, for she complained of "the winter of my discontent" when a chill January day brought illness. She admired the "parterres of flowers" at a hotel, rated the pronunciation at a dramatic reading "execrable in the extreme," and recalled Tennyson's description of ocean waves that "break, break, break on the cold gray stones." She enjoyed playing Logomachy, a Scrabble-like card game of the day. She used her knowledge in a way that was sharp, witty, and penetrating—generous to friends yet quick to take offense when she felt someone had broken the rules of etiquette or breached her moral code.

For indeed, the teachers at Shaw insisted that education be a moral experience, that knowledge be infused with belief, and that Christian behavior must always be decorous and above reproach. With this creed her mother agreed, and not merely out

Logomachy, a card game

of respect for the Victorian conventions of the day. Black women, Lizzie recognized, bore a special burden when it came to defining themselves in a post-emancipation world.

❦

Ida discovered this principle during one of her grandmother Peggy's annual visits. She brought cotton and corn to market from the country farm she and her husband owned. (She also brought along as gifts for the children hog bladders that could be inflated and popped in a most gratifying way.)[17] Sixty years later, Ida still remembered her ears burning when Grandmother Peggy, on one of these visits, commented that Miss Polly, her former mistress, had invited Jim to come home and show her his children.

"Mother, I never want to see that old woman as long as I live," Jim replied bitterly. "I'll never forget how she had you stripped and whipped the day after the old man died, and I am never going to see her." It was then that Ida discovered a timeless truth of human nature: when something is hidden in plain sight—a thing that cannot be discussed easily in public, yet is known to all—it often becomes simultaneously a matter of attraction and repulsion, fascination and horror.

Why would Miss Polly have her grandmother's clothes pulled off and the lash applied, merely because Miss Polly's husband had died? Ida was "burning to ask what he meant, but children were seen and not heard in those days. They didn't dare break into old folks' conversation." Especially when it hinted of questions so difficult to answer. How could Lizzie explain to her daughter why Peggy would have been humiliated in that way? Would Peggy even have confided to Lizzie the nature of her relationship with her former master? Was Jim born because she had been forced to submit to his attentions—raped, in short? Or had she grudgingly put up with her master's advances in return for better treatment—feigning attachment as a prostitute might? Or had some mutual affection developed between the two, despite the master's marriage to Miss Polly—and despite Peggy's marriage, apparently even before the war, to the black man who was now her lawful husband? In a devout family like Ida's, how might they explain that Jim Wells was an illegitimate son, fathered out of wedlock, whose lighter skin color and resemblance to his white father displayed to all the world this shameful state of affairs?

Such facts were in plain sight yet not easily spoken of in polite company. Life went on. What Ida did come to understand was that a double standard existed when it came to sexual liaisons between white men and black women. A white man was almost never blamed for such unions, which was why Miss Polly suffered in silence for so many years. Instead, the black woman was at fault—assumed to be the temptress, the seducer—which was why Peggy was whipped once Miss Polly's husband was in the grave. If ever a question arose regarding the propriety of a black woman's conduct, that woman was presumed guilty until proved innocent. In some folks' eyes "there were no virtuous southern [black] girls," Ida remarked acidly years later.

Lizzie knew that if she were going to protect her daughters, the moral component of their education would be vital. The Wells home served not only as a refuge from the former indecencies of slavery but also as a nursery of piety and decorum. In bondage Lizzie spent years in Spires Bolling's middle-class home. She knew how to run a proper household, and she prided herself on her discipline. Ida and the other children were taught from an early age to address their parents with respect. Each had assigned chores and were expected to keep their rooms orderly and clean. Ida learned, of course, how to sew, iron, and wash clothes; and felt the effects. A day's work at the washboard left her hands swollen.[18] She knew, too, how to dress neatly, to sit up "straight and proper," to pass behind a person rather than in front in polite company, to stand when superiors entered the room and remain standing until they sat, and never to eat food while walking on the street. Occasionally she might forget herself. "Came home early & found the elder awaiting me," she wrote in her diary. "On the impulse of the moment I simply bowed & passed thro, but recollecting myself I went back and shook hands with the gentleman."[19]

As for relations with the opposite sex, white or black, Lizzie knew Ida must be protected. White men were always ready to treat women "who have negro blood in their veins" as natural "prostitutes."[20] White men who preyed on black women justified their conduct with such rationalizations, and black mothers knew full well it could be dangerous for daughters to work in jobs that took them into white houses: doing laundry or housecleaning, for example.

Like young, middle-class white women, Ida learned the proper etiquette for dealing with men from Lizzie and her teachers at Shaw. She was careful to address acquaintances by their proper names—"Mr. Dardis" not "George," to present a calling card when visiting, to wear fashionable but not seductive clothing, to avoid being alone with a male friend in a room or in secluded areas.[21] In any case, Lizzie gave her daughter scant opportunity to break this elaborate code of conduct. At the age of sixteen, Ida "had never had a beau" and was "too young to have been out in company except at children's parties."[22]

That was as it should have been, Lizzie believed. Ida deserved the protected childhood her mother had never enjoyed as a slave. Both mother and daughter would have agreed with the black journalist who wrote, "every young woman's ambition is to have a home of her own," and "it makes no difference how much wealth, how much beauty you may possess, your brilliant talents, if you are void of the purity of purpose, nobleness of soul, you are not what God intended."[23] Lizzie's dedication to these ideals was so great that, taking her six children with her to every class, she won the prize for regular attendance at Sunday school.

Ida celebrated her sixteenth birthday in July 1878. A few weeks later, in a sign of her parents' growing trust, she was allowed to help grandmother Peggy and her husband harvest the first fall cotton at their farm. Unfortunately, soon after she arrived Ida came down with a mild case of malaria, common in those parts. She was alone in her grandmother's cabin, sweating off the fever, when she heard a hail from someone at the fence gate. She came to the door just as three men on horseback dismounted: friends of her parents, she recognized, from Holly Springs. Never mind the fever, when someone called, etiquette required that one stand and invite them in. Ida waited until they were seated before asking if they had any news from home. One of the men produced a letter, which she began reading eagerly. She got no further than the first page before a sentence leapt out that set her head spinning far more than the malarial sweats had. Her legs buckled beneath her and she fell to the floor senseless.

❧——❧

When speculation over the unknown fuels the known, rumors spark fear—especially when what *is* known is fearsome enough. In 1878 Memphis knew about yellow fever. Five years earlier two thousand residents died when an epidemic swept the city, and Memphis had experienced other bouts of smallpox, cholera, typhus, and scarlet fever.

Like malaria, yellow fever afflicted its victims with fever and chills, but the symptoms were more violent, accompanied by excruciating headaches and severe back pain. In many cases, sufferers felt better after a few days, encouraging hope that the danger had passed. All too often, however, the body temperature dropped again, the pulse became rapid, and massive kidney and liver failure caused bleeding from almost any opening of the body—even the pores—while the skin itself turned yellow. Wracked by nausea, patients vomited up black blood and soon died. The sickness proved most fatal to adults in the prime of their lives rather than to the old or young.

Rumors began circulating in May, with reports that "yellow jack" had returned to New Orleans from the Caribbean. But only at the end of July did officials there confirm that an epidemic was in progress. Immediately quarantine stations went up on rail lines into the city and on the Mississippi River as well to keep the infection out of Memphis. It was no use. City officials announced the death of an Italian snack-house keeper on August 14. Within two days another fifty-five people succumbed.

The news, following weeks of nervous speculation, provoked wholesale panic. A few folk scrambled onto steamboats to escape, but most knew better than to become trapped aboard "floating charnelhouses" where the epidemic could spread, and after which other towns would surely refuse to allow the boat to dock. Most escapes via the river were "by bateaux, by anything that could float," or on land by "carriages, buggies, wagons, furniture vans and street drays" and, of course, the railroads. Every train to Cincinnati was packed, the station platform mobbed. Men who lacked tickets used guns to force their way aboard. Others pried open the car windows and clambered in over ladies already seated. Train after train groaned down the tracks, to meet with armed guards at towns along the line, desperate to keep their own settlements free of the fever. In ten days, over twenty thousand left Memphis. Another five thousand walked out of the city every night to sleep in the countryside, since most people thought the disease was spread by the damp night air. Only about half the population remained, three-quarters of them African American, many of whom could not afford to get away.[24]

Not everyone's response was fear. Doctors from both the North and elsewhere in the South arrived in the city to tend the ill. Charitable organizations sent supplies and nurses, prime among them the Howard Association, which was particularly devoted to countering yellow fever. Annie Cook, the keeper of a renowned (or notorious) whorehouse on Gayoso Street, cleared her mansion to take in patients and died of the disease while caring for the sick.[25]

In Holly Springs, fifty miles to the south, a board of health was created to decide whether refugees should be allowed to enter. The town would be safe, the board concluded, as it was located on the highest ground in Mississippi, well above the "miasmas" of swamps. (The role of mosquitoes as disease carriers remained undiscovered for two more decades.) So the refugees came, and within a week the same horrific pattern repeated itself: death everywhere, two thousand fled out of thirty-five hundred residents. Only three hundred whites remained in town, along with twelve hundred blacks.[26]

Early word of the epidemic had already reached Ida, including the fact that the sickness had entered Holly Springs. But everyone at the farm was confident that her parents and siblings had fled to stay with Aunt Belle, another relative nearby.

They had not. Perhaps it had been too hard to pack up six children, which included Stanley, an infant less than a year old.

In addition their second-oldest child, Eugenia, had grown up afflicted with scoliosis, a paralyzing curvature of the spine that left her unable to walk. For whatever reason, Lizzie fell ill before flight could be arranged. Fever wracked her even as she continued to nurse Stanley, and all the children except 'Genie came down with mild cases of the disease. Jim stayed out of the home once Lizzie had taken to her bed, because if both parents died, who would support the family? During the day he went about his business, for the demand was high for carpenters to make coffins. At the end of each day he left a basket of food within reach of the yard gate, as he called in to learn how the family fared.

An Irish nurse tended Lizzie, and when the fever returned in strength, the nurse removed Stanley from his mother's breast. Lizzie's milk clotted, her fever spiked, and her condition worsened. She was tormented by the thought of leaving the children she had done so much to nourish. What would become of them, she asked? As death approached Jim returned to be with her. Almost immediately he was stricken too, more severely.

"They died within twenty-four hours of each other," the letter said. "The children are all at home and the Howard Association has put a woman there to take care of them. Send word to Ida." This was the news that caused her to faint.

Ida's instinct was to return immediately to Holly Springs, but the adults at the farm opposed the idea. She must wait until the epidemic passed. Three days later a letter arrived from Dr. Gray of the Howard Association—white, not a native of Holly Springs—saying the disease had abated and she should come. Grudgingly, Ida's uncle took her to the train station. Virtually everyone milling around there advised her to wait. This white doctor was from out of town, they insisted—he'd go back where he came from without a care for what became of Ida. Better to stay away. Reluctantly, Ida sat down and wrote a letter, saying she would come later. But she could not get her brothers and sisters out of her mind, and when the train pulled into the station, she put the letter aside and boarded herself.

It wasn't a passenger train, only a freight. No regular trains were running, for the simple reason that so many folk had fled. There was no business. The caboose, where Ida rode, was draped in black bunting. Two conductors in a row had braved the run during the past few weeks, and died. Their replacement eyed Ida suspiciously and wanted to know why she was venturing into town. "Why are *you?*" she countered. He shrugged. Somebody had to.

"That's exactly why I am going home," she told him. He bid her good-bye in Holly Springs, Ida recalled, "as though he never expected to see me again."

Fortunately the children were not without resources. Over the years Jim had managed to save $300, which 'Genie had asked Dr. Gray to hold for safekeeping. Ida went to the courthouse, now a makeshift hospital, to inquire for the money. "So you are 'Genie's big sister," Gray said. "Tell her the treasurer has the key to the safe and will be back this evening. I will bring her the money tonight, as I am leaving tomorrow." Jim had been a help to the end, he assured her. "If he passed a patient who was out of his head, he would stop to quiet him. If he were dying, he would kneel down and pray with him, then pick up his tools and go on with the day's work."

The community also provided support. Wells was a Mason, and friends in that organization convened a meeting to decide how best to help the family. The discussion lasted most of the afternoon. Ida, they decided, was old enough to fend for herself. The wives of two black Masons were each willing to adopt one younger sister, for they wanted daughters. Two other Masons, one white, agreed to apprentice the Wells boys as carpenters. No one spoke up for 'Genie who, being paralyzed, offered little prospect of economic benefit. She would have to go to the poorhouse. Ida listened in silence.

For a second time the stubborn streak showed. Her parents would "roll over in their graves" to see the family split so, she announced. As a child, her mother had been sold at auction and her own family separated. If the Masons could help find a job, Ida promised, she would undertake to provide for her siblings. The house in Holly Springs was paid for, free and clear. They could live there. The Masons "scoffed" at this notion, but Ida held firm. At last they agreed, and after some discussion decided that teaching offered the most likely source of income for the young girl. Ida had not yet received her degree from Shaw, but the qualifying exams for country schools were less rigorous than those in towns and cities.

Ida soon found that getting a living was not the only hurdle to clear. In town tongues had begun to wag, spurred on by what some witnessed on the courthouse square. That young black girl was talking to a white Northerner. She was asking for money. And now she was setting up in a house of her own, without anyone proper to watch her. Why else would a black girl live unchaperoned while soliciting money from white men? *They say*. Ida was taken aback. It would not be the last time such questions were asked.

❧—❧

She adjusted. Grandmother Peggy, in her seventies, came in from the country to live with the youngsters once Ida got a job.

Then she lowered the hemlines of her skirts to the level worn by adults and began a daunting schedule: ride, mule back, six miles into the country on Sunday afternoon in order to be ready for class Monday morning; instruct a wide variety of students in the basics of reading, writing, and arithmetic in a crowded, one-room school; stay at one lodging or another weeknights, on a salary that provided not even money enough for candles to read by at night. (The blaze of a fire had to serve.) Return home by mule Friday evening to greet Peggy and the children, with eggs and butter donated by the parents of her students. The weekend was for washing, ironing, and darning the children's clothes. In the summer, when school let out, she returned to Shaw, working toward the degree she had been striving so long for.[27]

The details of what happened next—sometime around 1880 or 1881—will likely never be known. Ida found the episode too painful to speak of in detail. For some reason, W. W. Hooper, the president of Shaw, ordered her expelled.

Hooper was a devout man, severe at times. It was said that at daily services he prayed with his eyes open, voice echoing across the room. Jesus insisted that God allowed not even a single sparrow to fall to the ground without his say so. Hooper, emulating the Father, watched his own sparrows like a hawk. Ida did something that angered him, whether in chapel or out. When called to account, she defended herself and refused to back down or apologize.

Five years later—long after she secured a reputable teaching position in Memphis—she returned to Shaw. A friend was being married around the time of graduation. Hooper performed the wedding rites and was pleasant enough with Ida. The bride was a particular favorite of the president's; as a student Ida suspected that this favor resulted from lighter skin color. Even many of the Northern missionaries seemed to prefer the lighter-skinned mulattos. But, Ida confessed to her diary,

> I decided that it was not—as I used to think in my childish rage & jealousy at his evident preference for her—because of her color (for there have been others who were brighter in color and withal prettier than she and yet who won not his favor); it was not her high intellectual powers (for many I know were more brilliant…) and so I've come to the conclusion that it was her obedient disposition, her extreme tractableness and therefore easily controlled and her evident ladylike refinement and where I think of my tempestuous, rebellious, hard headed wilfulness, the trouble I gave, the disposition to question his authority—I remember that Mr. H[ooper] is but human and I no longer cherish feelings of resentment, nor blame him that my scholastic career was cut short; my own experience as a teacher enables me to see more clearly and I know that I was to blame.

Five years after being expelled it was easier to step back and analyze her own character. She was by no means a "tractable" woman—not when she defied her relatives and took the train toward the yellow fever epidemic, not when she opposed the Masons who decided to break up the family of a former slave, not when she resisted a school president who preferred his black girls to be yielding and obedient.

At commencement ceremonies, with President Hooper standing there in front of her, it was harder to step back. Ida watched the graduates recite their exercises and one by one stand up to receive their degrees. Such pride in mastering their lessons, without resorting to vine-covered schools in the woods or to stealing lessons from the alphabet blocks of a young mistress! For Ida, the

Wells around 1893

pomp and circumstance proved too potent. "As I witnessed the triumph of the graduates and thought of my lost opportunity a great sob arose in my throat and I yearned with unutterable long-ing for the 'might have been.' When [a friend] said to me after-ward: 'Ida, you ought to come back here and graduate,' I could not restrain my tears at the sense of injustice I felt, and begged him not to ask me why I said 'I could not.' I quickly conquered that feeling and as heartily wished the graduates joy as tho' no bitterness had mingled with my pleasure."[28]

As though. Ida might wish for decorum and very often achieve it. When it came to matters of the heart, however, and issues of principle, she refused to be tractable.

· Three ·

UNLADYLIKE LADY

❦——❧

ABOUT THE TIME OF HER DISMISSAL FROM SHAW—PERHAPS even partly because of it—an invitation arrived that changed Ida's life once again.[1] Yellow fever had left her an orphan, a stand-in parent, and her family's primary breadwinner. Relatives and friends pulled together, of course, as they often do in times of trouble. Grandmother Peggy watched the children while Ida taught in the country. When Peggy was felled by a stroke, one of Lizzie's old friends stepped in. Aunt Belle, Lizzie's sister, agreed to care for 'Genie, paralyzed from scoliosis. But for over two years the burden of worry, if not of constant supervision, fell to Ida.

The invitation came sometime in 1881—from Aunt Fannie Butler, her father's stepsister. Aunt Fannie suggested Ida come to Memphis. Fannie had lost her husband to the yellow fever epidemic, just as Ida had lost her parents. Living together would ease housing costs and provide companionship—not only for Ida and Fanny—but for Annie and Lily, Ida's two younger sisters, who could play with Fannie's children. (Ida's brothers, Jim and George, had by this time apprenticed themselves out as carpenters' assistants.)[2]

The move made sense for other reasons. Memphis was a magnet for African Americans—from western Tennessee, northern Mississippi, and not least from Holly Springs. The Reverend Africa Bailey, a former Marshall County slave, had become pastor of a Baptist church in the city near Fort Pickering, where thousands of slaves fled to enlist in the Union Army.[3] Others from Holly Springs, like Ida's older friend Alfred Froman, the owner of a saddle shop, went into business in Memphis. Even more well known was Robert R. Church, Sr., born a slave in Holly Springs by a white father, as Jim Wells had been. Young Church worked for a time as a cabin boy and steward (his father owned several steamboats) and by 1866 was the owner of a Memphis grocery store and saloon.

It was in that year that white rioters, many of them Irish workers who resented the newly independent African American soldiers, rampaged through black neighborhoods. While guarding his saloon, Church was shot in the back of the head and left for dead. Miraculously he survived, but for the rest of his life he was afflicted periodically by excruciating headaches. And the bullet hole remained, "into which one could easily insert the tip of the little finger," his daughter reported.[4]

When thousands fled the yellow fever epidemic in 1878, Church was among the many African Americans who stayed. In the wake of the crisis he bought up real estate that seemed worthless in a half-empty city. As Memphis recovered, Church's shrewd investments made him very wealthy and he used his wealth to underwrite the black community: founding a bank, building a park and auditorium, as well as buying city bonds at a time when most investors remained skittish. Some years later he loaned Ida money that she badly needed for a cross-country train fare, though he did not know her well.[5]

Church was only the most prominent figure among the burgeoning network of African Americans who helped one another make Memphis a tolerable place to live. The poorest shared, out of necessity. Around Fort Pickering, where black soldiers first housed their wives and children, as many as seven families squeezed into the living quarters of a four- to five-room house. Clothing was so scarce that soldiers gave wives parts of their uniforms.[6] Over the next decade, newcomers worked in a host of unskilled positions. Perhaps a quarter of African American residents held skilled jobs, becoming pastors, physicians, bricklayers, barbers, and more.[7] From their earnings, workers of all sorts donated to charitable organizations, especially black churches.

Beale Street Baptist, one of the oldest churches, was the chief recipient. To begin with, the congregation was so poor that it was obliged to meet in brush arbors—canopies of leaves and branches held aloft on log poles, thrown up at the corner of Beale and Lauderdale streets. With so many freedpeople arriving in Memphis, the church grew by leaps and bounds, along with the donations in the collection plate. On some occasions so much change came in that members had to count it on a large table, then deposit it into tubs for storage, using shovels.[8] By 1871 the congregation had collected enough to lay the cornerstone for a grand new church.

During Reconstruction, more than two hundred charitable groups opened savings accounts at the city's Freedmen's Savings and Trust Company, to help black citizens with everything from emergency assistance (the Sons and Daughters of Zion, the Hospital Fund of the Colored Sons of Temperance) to burial expenses (Union Forever). The bank held the savings of a college drama group, an emigration association for those considering a move to Africa, and fraternal organizations like the Sons of Ham.[9]

So when Ida left Holly Springs with Annie and Lily in tow, she was not heading into the unknown, or moving in without support. Still, the journey must have been tinged with apprehension as well as excitement. The rail route crossed Pontotoc Ridge, on which Holly Springs stood, and descended through rolling country and forests of magnolia and pine, hickory and oak, as well as fields of cotton. From Redbanks, about ten miles away, the clock tower of the Holly Springs courthouse could still be glimpsed, but as the train continued its downward path, the pleasant country gave way more often to rough gullies of red clay and then crossed into Tennessee, where Memphis spread out along the bluffs of the broad Mississippi.[10] Even though the city had lost half of its population after the epidemic, it was ten times the size of Holly Springs. Over the next two decades, nearly seventy thousand more folk would come, both black and white, tripling its size.

Ida, a year shy of twenty, had a lot to take in. The central thoroughfare for most African Americans was Beale Street, which had its beginning at the DeSoto Fish Dock. There, boats brought in the day's catch, making their way past the steamboats tied up along the river. These stern- and side-wheelers took on passengers of all sorts as well as hundreds upon hundreds of bales of cotton, hauled to water's edge by black draymen. (In market season, from October to January, the bales were piled high along the streets.)[11] A number of African American entrepreneurs did well for themselves by running a fleet of drays, carts used to haul cotton, lumber, and every kind of freight.[12] At lunchtime and dinner,

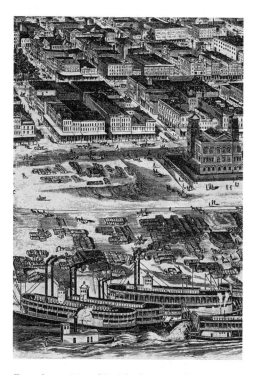

*Front Street, Memphis, (also known as "Front Row")
can be seen near the top of this engraving done around
1891. The street ran along the levee overlooking the
docks at which steamboats loaded freight.*

the burly stevedores who loaded the boats came striding up Beale
Street, talking, laughing, looking for a plate of fried catfish or a
shot of whiskey, their trousers rolled to their knees and their cotton hooks—used to manhandle the bales—stuck in their belts.[13]

Up from the dock were several blocks devoted to black-owned businesses—groceries and saloons, clothing stores, doctors' offices, photographers, insurance agents, pawnshops, and barbers. An open-air market offered vegetables and fruits sold from stalls, as well as goods laid out on blankets and hawked by vendors. As Beale Street crossed Hernando, less reputable shops and saloons began to appear, in an area coming to be known as the "black magic" district. There, witch doctors skilled in the arts of voodoo told fortunes or offered "luck bags" to hang around the neck. Others peddled passion flowers, love potions, or even graveyard dust, intended to benefit the lives and loves of those who bought them or to thwart the designs of enemies. Ida had neither time nor patience for such superstitions, but only a block farther, at the corner of DeSoto, loomed the twin towers of the new Beale Street Baptist Church. Atop one tower a statue of John the Baptist stood, his arm extended heavenward toward salvation.[14]

Ida had never before worshiped in a sanctuary of such magnificence, where more than two thousand faithful might assemble on a Sunday; and Beale was only first among many.[15] By the time she arrived, Memphis boasted more black than white Protestant churches.[16] Ida often attended Avery Chapel, the African Methodist Episcopal Church (AME) founded by black Union veterans. As she got to know a variety of churches in the city, she gravitated increasingly toward Vance Street Christian Church.[17] But Ida hardly confined her activities to a single congregation. She might attend morning worship at Beale Street Baptist, or perhaps Immanuel Episcopal, where Robert Church was a member, then return to Avery to teach Sunday school in the afternoon, and

Beale Street Baptist Church. The statue of John the Baptist, atop the left tower, no longer exists. According to historian Beverly G. Bond, the statue was frequently struck by lightning and once disfigured by a drunken intruder.

after supper head out to Collins Chapel, a branch of the more socially elite Colored Methodist Episcopal Church (CME).[18] On another Sunday she might take communion at the Second Congregational Church or on a weekday enjoy a church fair at the LeMoyne Institute. Very occasionally she managed four events on a single Sunday.

Nor did she hesitate to worship at white churches. When the charismatic three-hundred-pound revival preacher Dwight Moody came to town, she heard him not only at Avery Chapel but also from the front of the segregated gallery at Cumberland Presbyterian Church. She praised Moody's style for being "so simple, plain, and natural. He told the old, old story in an easy conversational way that charms the listener ere he is aware and the secret of his success is, I think—that he does not preach a far-away God—a hard to be reconciled Saviour but uses a natural earnest tone and tells in a natural way without any long drawn doctrine or finely spun theology or rhetoric the simple truth that Christ Jesus came on earth to seek & save that which was lost." Despite Moody's virtues she was sorely tempted to write him asking why he and other white ministers "never touched on that phase of sin—the caste distinction [of segregation]—practised even in the churches and among christianity(?) but rather, tacitly conniving at it…and accepting it as a matter of course, instead of rectifying it." Such behavior she totted up as "practical evidence of 'white folks' Christianity." On the other hand, during a series of speeches dedicating a new school she "was agreeably surprised by a rare treat from Rabbi Samfield. It's the first time I ever heard a Jewish intellectual discourse."[19]

Getting to these services, as well as to shops and businesses, could prove a challenge in Memphis. Walking was always an option, though a winter storm might leave her "utterly exhausted with wading thro' the snow" or ice make the pavements "so glassy…we were afraid to venture."[20] But in 1881, the sidewalks in Memphis were hardly universal, and most of the city streets were only graveled. Sprinkler wagons drove around in summer to keep down the dust. Twenty years earlier a dozen miles of downtown had been done over in Nicholson pavement, a treated hardwood, but that surface quickly rotted, leaving the streets pockmarked with stagnant water.[21] Ida often paid a nickel to ride the city streetcars, pulled along iron rails by a single mule or a pair.[22] At least once she rode horseback for pleasure, though her mount, she reported, "was afraid of the streetcars, & the first one I met, he ran up on the mules & began rearing and plunging. I was terribly frightened but kept my seat until we got a little to one side, when the horse's leg became entangled in the traces & that threw him and I went over his back."[23]

Along Main Street, the shops dwarfed any in Holly Springs, particularly Menken's "Palatial Emporium," a five-story brick marvel that boasted "Thirty Stores Under One Roof."[24] Ida established an account and over the coming years found herself resisting the temptation to add to her bill for furniture, vases, shoes, dresses, cloaks, gloves, and the makings for clothing that she sewed or trimmed herself: thread, lace, buttons, and silk or other fabrics. She was also a regular customer at Williams's bookstore, both to satisfy her voracious reading habits and for stationery to undertake her considerable correspondence.

Beyond the frequent church socials and services, Ida could attend lectures at the Knights of Labor or the LeMoyne Normal Institute for Teachers, or ponder a talk on Africa by Christian missionaries. There was baseball. "Saw a professional game for the first time," she reported, "but lost my temper & acted in an unladylike way toward those in whose company I was."[25] Theaters offered high dramas and low comedies, not all to her taste. "I went to the theatre with Ella & Boots, to see 'Humbug' & humbug it was." On the other hand, Gilbert and Sullivan's wildly popular musical, *The Mikado*, charmed her. "It is a delightful jumble of ridiculous and laughable; a comic combination of songs, speeches, and actions, and dress; for everything is represented as Japanese. It is very bright and sparkling, with no suggestion of the coarse or vulgar; the character of Ko-Ko is inimitable & it was acted to perfection."[26] Delightful fantasy! To think that Ko-Ko, a disreputable tailor of no social standing, could become the Lord High Executioner, turning the social ladder on its head while singing clever ditties:

> Wafted by a favouring gale,
> As one sometimes is in trances,
> To a height that few can scale,
> Save by long and weary dances.

The end of Reconstruction eliminated any fantasy that the South would turn the social ladder on its head, or create a political order in which blacks stood on equal footing with whites, even after long and weary dances. Still, for a generation of freedpeople looking to carve out new identities, Memphis was not the worst place in the world to live. The city directory of 1870 listed African Americans in a remarkably wide variety of occupations:

Barber, Pastor, Engineer, Plasterer, Express Cartman, Boot and Shoemaker, Porter, Laborer, Cook, Painter, Washing, Blacksmith, Drayman, Foundry Moulder, Brick Layer, Druggist, Physician, Surgeon, Steamboatman, Cotton Picker, Brickmason, Stonecutter, Baker, Fireman, Woodhauler, Teamster, Shinglemaker, Striker, Waterdrawer, Harnessmaker, Gardener, Brakeman, Hand Expressmaker, Brickmoulder, Whitewasher, Mattressmaker, Upholsterer, Varnisher, Cotton Planter, Farmer, Boardinghouse, Eating House,

A trade card from the 1880s featuring The Mikado's Koko while also advertising J & P Coats sewing thread

Buggywasher, Coachman, Sailor, Bookmaker, Cooper, Hatter, Riverporter, Confectioner, Basketmaker, Lamplighter, Wiper, Carriage Painter, Ragpicker, Waiter, Cistern Builder, Sexton, Machinist, Mailgatherer, Riverfireman, Saloon Keeper, Cupola-man, Grocer, Broommaker, Bartender.[27]

Ida had her own ambitions, now that she was in Memphis. According to those who knew her, they included becoming "a full-fledged journalist, a physician, or an actress."[28] Why not? Who could guess, like Ko-Ko, where a "favouring gale" might waft?

❧—◆—❧

In 1881, Miss Ida B. Wells belonged to none of these professions. She was a teacher and proud of it, even if the work could be frustrating. Her pupils addressed her as Miss Wells, as did her male and female colleagues. That was a badge of freedom, after all. For two hundred years, whites had called adult slaves by their first names, as if they were still children, or bestowed patronizing names like Cuffee and Cicero. Like other middle-class folk, if Wells went visiting and no one was home, she left a calling card, with her name engraved as she preferred it: Miss Ida B. Wells.[29]

Moving to Memphis, Ida obtained a job at a school in Woodstock, a town a dozen miles north of the city. Every week she got to classes by riding the Chesapeake, Ohio, and Southwestern Railroad. The C&O schedules were regular enough. But it was hard to anticipate from week to week the reception she might receive on board the train.

A lot depended on which car she rode. Trains usually pulled two. The one directly behind the engine was the smoking car, also known as second class, where conditions were far from ideal. Tobacco fumes filled the air and those riders who chewed instead of smoked habitually ignored the spittoons and showered the floor with tobacco juice. Nor was smoke the only pollutant. Because the car sat directly behind the locomotive, engine ash and soot were much more likely to drift in the doors. In winter, heat was provided by a wood stove whose legs were screwed down and sides braced against the wall, to keep hot coals from jostling onto the floor. In summer, a difficult choice had to be made: whether to shut the windows and suffocate or open them and be showered by cinders.[30]

Since the smoker held the cheapest seats, the people using them were often a rougher crowd. Tobacco was the least of the vices to be endured, for men brought along pints of whiskey and amply indulged their thirsts. Swearing and arguing were common. "The cars were jammed, all the way over here, with the dirtiest, nastiest set I ever rode with," complained one traveler.[31] Immigrant families with baggage also crowded in, traveling on discounted rates.[32]

First-class accommodations could be had in what was known as the ladies' car. Men were sometimes permitted if they maintained a proper decorum and did not smoke, though often only if they were also escorting a woman. Most of these cars boasted a water cooler, carpets on the floor, and upholstered seating. The surroundings were desirable enough that one male passenger, traveling alone, sued the railroad after being refused a seat in first class. The foul air in the smoker was likely to make him ill, he insisted.[33]

For Ida the choice was clear: buy first-class tickets. But whether she could use them was a question that had become increasingly complicated in the early 1880s. Leaving her lodgings at Aunt Fannie's she could catch a streetcar to the railroad depot, sitting side by side with whites without arousing any remark or protest. Streetcars were integrated in major Southern cities beginning after the war. ("Let's have our rights!" yelled the crowd of freedpeople who led the way in Richmond.)[34] But the situation on railroads was different, and the law on the matter was conflicted and changing.

As Reconstruction waned, the Republican Congress passed the Civil Rights Act of 1875. It declared that "citizens of every race and color" were "entitled to the full and equal enjoyment of the accommodations, advantages, facilities, and privileges of inns, public conveyances on land or water, theaters, and other places of public amusement."[35] That statute reinforced a similar Tennessee law established in 1867. But the same year that Congress passed the Civil Rights Act, Tennessee replaced its older law with a new one that decreed hotels, public halls, and transportation companies could refuse to serve "any person" for any reason whatever.[36] In short, facilities could segregate their operations simply by barring all blacks.

In 1881, the year Wells arrived in Memphis, the four African Americans remaining in the state legislature made a bid to repeal Tennessee's law. Their effort failed, but white legislators offered a compromise. Railroads would be required to provide first-class "colored" accommodations, although the facilities could be separate from ones used by whites. Did such a law provide "full and equal enjoyment" of public transportation by all races? Many whites thought so. "*Equal* accommodations do not mean *identical* accommodations," one Tennessee judge explained.[37]

Once the new law was in place, some railroads occasionally added a third car to their trains, designated as "first-class colored." Even so, whites could sit there too if the rest of the cars were crowded, and the rules against smoking, drinking, or swearing were never enforced. Most trains had no third car and then, when blacks took seats in the ladies car, the reception they received depended on the character of the conductor, the mood of white patrons, or the resolve of the black passenger.

A black woman riding first class on the Memphis and Charleston Railroad, described as "proper" by white observers, was asked by the conductor to leave. Rather than retreat to the smoker, where there was "swearing and smoking and whiskey drinking," the woman got off at the next station.[38] Mary Church, the daughter of Memphis businessman Robert R. Church, was five years old and sitting alone in the ladies car while her father was off briefly for a smoke. A conductor came along and demanded to know "Whose little nigger is this?" He began escorting her out just as Church returned. Seeing his daughter about to be ejected, he pulled out his revolver. "There ensued a scene which no one who saw it could ever forget," recalled Mary delicately. She and her father remained in first class.[39] A black man named Murphy traveling from Georgia to Tennessee was not so lucky. He rode first class without any objections for a time, until two white women boarded along with their male escorts. The white men told Murphy to leave, and when he refused, they carried him out bodily and threw him into the smoking car.[40]

African Americans strongly believed that the Civil Rights Act guaranteed them first-class seats when first-class tickets were purchased. Jane Brown, who was thrown off the Memphis and Charleston Railroad, was awarded the substantial sum of $3,000 in damages by a federal court.[41] When Tennessee put in place its

1881 law calling for separate first-class facilities, several black citizens in Nashville challenged the new rules. For three days they bought first-class tickets and attempted to board the usual cars. The railroads, unsure of their legal ground, attempted an end-run—literally. When black passengers arrived to take ladies-car seats, white passengers were taken off and locked into their own separate car, safe from racial mixing. The following day, when the protesters returned early and discovered conductors performing the same diversion, they followed the whites to the other car—whereupon the whites hurried back into the original ladies car and were locked in there.

Such evasions disheartened blacks, who insisted that *separate but equal* was not the same as *equal*. Yet during the railroad's elaborate game of cat-and-mouse, at least none of the Nashville protesters had been ejected. A white newspaper editor there refused to attach great importance to the dispute. If the courts decided that blacks paying first class had "the right to any seat…it will be of no more consequence to anybody than the right he has exercised for years in the street cars," he argued.[42] In 1882, after Ida had begun working in Woodstock, one railroad settled out of court for $700 with a black woman who had been ejected despite her first-class ticket.[43]

What did all the maneuvering mean? Everything and nothing, from week to week. Ida never knew whether she would be accepted without comment, glared at and cross-examined, thrown off the car, or allowed to stay if she argued strongly enough. It did sometimes seem a matter of bluff. But how far should one go, if push came literally to shove? Ida's mother and her instructors at Shaw University had all insisted on the importance of being "ladylike."

Anna Julia Cooper, a Southern black woman only a little older than Wells, described the "feeling of slighted womanhood" upon being harassed in the ladies car. The natural "first impulse," she explained, was one of "wrathful protest and proud self vindication." But the moment a lady stood up to demand her rights, such feelings were "checked and shamed by the consciousness that self assertion would outrage still further the same delicate instinct."[44] Being a lady, would it not be better to remain silent?

One Saturday evening in 1883 Miss Wells found out. She boarded the ladies car as usual, wearing her linen duster, a fashionable lightweight coat designed to protect her dress against the hazards of travel. She also carried baggage for the week and an umbrella.

Once the passengers had boarded, the train lurched into motion, proceeding out of the C&O depot along the bluff above the Mississippi, whose mud flats and broad expanses stretched toward the Arkansas marshes on the far shore. Almost immediately the rail line veered to follow the much slower Wolf River, a stagnant tributary whose odors penetrated the cars when the windows were open.[45] The conductor worked his way down the aisle. Ida had brought something to read. Given her harried schedule, every free moment was precious. When the conductor approached, she handed him her ticket.

"I can't take this here," he said, returning it.

Ida looked up, retrieved the ticket, and returned to her reading. Years later she remembered thinking, "If he doesn't want it I won't bother about it."

Perhaps. Then again, perhaps she knew very well what he meant. If you went on with your business, the man might think better of the situation. No one was without a seat. Ida would be getting off at Woodstock, only a few miles up the line. He'd seen her ticket. If she behaved like a lady and just ignored him…

The conductor studied her and then proceeded to the next customer. The moment passed. The train snaked its way beyond the city limits.

A bit later Ida looked up to see he was back. This time, without a word, the conductor picked up her baggage and umbrella and headed for the smoking car. Wells knew there was trouble.

"I will treat you like a lady," he said when he returned. "But you will have to go to the other car."

She had no plan. She hadn't debated in her own mind where the boundary might lie between the silence of "slighted womanhood" and the act of insisting on her rights. Things just happened. *They say*—in this case, who was a lady and who was not. She had to respond.

"If you wish to treat me like a lady, you'll leave me alone," she replied. "The forward car is a smoker. This is the ladies car."

The conductor moved toward her. Ida braced against the seat ahead and held on.

The conductor grabbed her arm and tried to wrench her into the aisle. The white passengers nearby turned and gawked. He pulled harder; her duster tore. Ida leaned over and bit his hand as hard as she could. The conductor jumped back, hand bleeding.

Once the shock had registered the conductor disappeared down the aisle and in a moment returned with the baggage attendant and a third man. Some of the white passengers were calling encouragement to the conductor; others stood on their seats, to get a better view of the fracas. Ida braced again, but a few passengers moved the seat she was pushing against, and with three men pulling at her there was no contest. They maneuvered her into the aisle.

The train was slowing for its first stop, St. Elmo. Ida could see the smoking car looming ahead, crowded and hazy, where they meant to take her. She announced she would get off rather than submit to second-class treatment. Unceremoniously the men deposited her on the station platform with umbrella and baggage, to the cheers of the white passengers.

Furious and humiliated, she watched the train gain a new head of steam and chug on down the line. The sleeves of her duster had been pulled out. She found that somehow, despite the rough handling, she was still gripping her first-class ticket.[46]

❧——❧

The only black lawyer in Memphis that Wells knew was Thomas F. Cassells, also a member of the state legislature. She retained him to sue the C&O in state court. Federal court was no longer an option because several cases already brought under the Civil Rights Act had been appealed to the Supreme Court, which ruled in 1883 that the act could not prevent individuals or private corporations from discriminating against African Americans. Under Tennessee law, though, Wells could argue that the railroad had not provided her with separate facilities that were equal.

Tennessee Circuit Court judge James O. Pierce, a Union veteran from Minnesota, heard the case. He was more sympathetic than some judges in the system. To Wells's satisfaction, he ruled in May 1884 that her arguments were sound and awarded her $200. The railroad appealed.

Predictably Wells vowed to continue fighting, but the C&O embarked on strategy of delay. Months dragged by with nothing done. More disturbing, even her own lawyer seemed unenthusiastic. Why fight the appeal, Cassells asked. The railroad assured him personally that she "would not be disturbed any more." Ida suspected that the C&O had bought Cassells off. She would have none of it. Henceforth she directed a white lawyer, James Greer, to handle the case.

In the meantime, Wells had applied for a job in the Memphis public schools. The city's black population was growing steadily and the city schools offered better pay. She began teaching in Memphis in 1884, at which point she no longer took the train to Woodstock every week.

She did continue to visit friends, though, and despite the promise not to "disturb" her, another C&O conductor prevented Wells from entering the ladies car. The face-off was much like the sidewalk encounters of Mrs. Gill and her schoolchildren in Holly Springs. Wells produced her first-class ticket and tried to pass, but the man physically blocked her. Since the train was just leaving the station, the conductor called a halt. This time she disembarked without a struggle. But she promptly entered a second suit, charging not only discrimination but assault, since the conductor had "put his hands upon her to push her back and did do so."[47]

Again, Judge Pierce heard the case. He dismissed the assault charge but agreed that Wells had been discriminated against. "Although the professed rule was that no smoking, drunkenness or vulgar conduct was allowed" in the first-class car for colored people, he ruled, "still the actual allowance of smoking and drunkenness in that car reduced it below the grade of first-class."

The facilities provided were separate, but not equal. Pierce issued a second judgment against the railroad, this one for $500.[48]

That got the attention of the white press. On Christmas Day 1884 the *Memphis Daily Appeal* announced:

A DARKY DAMSEL

Obtains a Verdict for Damages Against
the Chesapeake and Ohio Railroad—What It Cost
To Put a Colored School-Teacher in a
Smoking Car—Verdict for
$500.[49]

The C&O lawyer, Holmes Cummins, immediately appealed the new decision and again worked diligently to delay. The facts seemed abundantly clear that Wells had been taken from the first-class car where no smoking was allowed and offered second-class accommodations in which smoking and drinking were abundant. As her lawyers pointed out on appeal, some blacks were indeed allowed in the first-class car (without complaint), so long as they were nurses tending white babies. This had the topsy-turvy effect of permitting lower-class African Americans to occupy first-class cars, while requiring middle- and upper-class blacks, who bought first-class tickets, to accept inferior conditions.[50]

The rest of 1885 passed without the court hearing the case. Clearly the railroad was nervous. Two decisions had been rendered in Wells's favor, and if upheld, they would establish a precedent that none of the railroads wanted. Cummins approached Wells and offered to settle out of court. If it was money she wanted…

Wells did need money—and rather urgently. Months went by sometimes before the school board paid its teachers. The moment Ida received an installment, she parceled it out to her various creditors. "I cannot consult a physician till I get some money," she confessed in January 1886. "If I once get out of debt I hope this lesson will be remembered and profited by: to think I am in debt more than one month's salary & if anything should happen I have not more than enough money coming to me to cancel my expenses." Despite such strains, she "indignantly" refused Holmes Cummins's offer to settle, as it would only put her "a few hundred dollars to the good." She still owed about $200 in court costs.[51]

Then in April a trusted friend warned Ida of "a conspiracy" against her that was "on foot to quash the case." Apparently the railroad tried to hire someone—older, and of considerable reputation—to seduce Wells. If the plot had succeeded, the C&O could threaten to expose the relationship unless she dropped the suit. A month later her friend and adviser Alfred Froman confirmed "the dirty method Mr. Cummins is attempting." Froman was well connected in political circles and took no guff from anyone. (He had distinguished himself fighting in the Massachusetts Fifty-fifth during the Civil War.) Confronting Cummins, Froman "ordered him to stop it," Ida noted. And the *Cleveland Gazette,* a black paper, reported the same attempt, presumably, "to put up a blackmailing job...to tarnish the character of the fair prosecutrix."[52]

"It is a painful fact that white men choose men of the [black] race to accomplish the ruin of any young girl," Wells wrote, alluding to the incident, "but that one would deliberately ask a man of reputation to encompass the ruin of one's reputation for the sake of gain is a startling commentary on the estimation in which our race is held." She knew all too well that the press was full of such "estimations," not merely in sensational newspapers but in staid, respectable journals. The "ties that bind the family together" were "relatively feeble…among these African people," commented Nathaniel Shaler in the *Atlantic Monthly*. "What we call morality…has no independent lodgment whatever in the native African breast," agreed the Reverend J. L. Tucker of Jackson, Mississippi. Emancipation had produced a "great descent into evil" and "a relapse into many practices of African barbarism." The *Encyclopaedia Britannica* listed Jackson in 1884 as an expert on the behavior of African Americans. "Chastity is a virtue which [black] parents do not seem anxious to foster," explained Philip A. Bruce, a Harvard law graduate, in the *New York Evening Post*. "Lasciviousness has done more than all the other vices of the plantation negro united to degrade" not merely field hands but the black "delegate who sits in the legislature, the teacher who has graduated from college, the preacher who has studied the Bible."[53]

For those holding such views it made little difference how much knowledge a black teacher might have gained or how meticulously she had been schooled in morals by her parents. She was a "darky damsel." If lasciviousness was an inbred trait, surely the Wells girl could be ensnared in immoral behavior? Or so Mr. Holmes Cummins hoped.

And if entrapment failed, there were the usual strategies of delay. For whatever reason, the case again was put off. Wells had to wait until 1887 for the court's final decision.

In the meantime she discovered that there were others—black as well as white—who wished to define how a free, young black woman should behave.

· *Four* ·

EDGED TOOLS

➤——

As the year 1887 opened, the Tennessee papers were filled with the sordid details of "the Godwin case," a cheerless tale of infidelity similar to so many that preoccupied the press, yet "shocking" for what it revealed "concerning the morals of high life," Miss Ida B. Wells noted in her diary. "A silly woman forgot her marriage vows for an equally scatterbrained boy; who boasted of his conquest in Nashville, St. Louis, Marianna, as well as here." Revenge was swift. The woman's brother murdered the lover who had been so casual in demeaning his sister's honor. Wells was horrified, yet of two minds about the crime. "It seems awful to take human life but hardly more so than to take a woman's reputation & make it the jest & byword of the street; in view of these things, if he really did them, one is strongly tempted to say his killing was justifiable."[1]

Justifiable homicide? These people were strangers to Wells—upper-class white folk, scatterbrained, revelers in the "high life" who inhabited a social universe distant from her own. For all that, the case hit a little too close to home. None of the accusations hurled against blacks stung "so deeply and keenly as the taunt of immorality," she wrote at the time of the scandal, "the jest and sneer with which our women are spoken of, and the utter incapacity or refusal to believe there are among us mothers, wives, and maidens who have attained a true, noble, and refining womanhood." Her good name was all she had in the world, she insisted years later. "I was bound to protect it from attack by those who felt that they could do so with impunity because I had no brother or father to protect it for me."[2]

There had been the incident in Holly Springs with Dr. Gray, of course, after the yellow fever epidemic. Speak with a white man and immediately gossips suggested she was setting herself up as a prostitute. Other rumors kept springing up. When Wells brought her younger sister to Memphis, tongues wagged that Lily was really her illegitimate daughter. When a fellow schoolteacher courted her, acquaintances in Kansas City whispered that the two had been fired for immoral conduct.[3] To hear such tattle made Ida "furiously angry." Even worse, the latter two accusations had been spread by black men, not whites. *They say*—one way or another.

Beyond relying on a brother or father to defend one's honor, the only remedy was constant vigilance. To mature and thrive as a free, black, educated woman demanded a scrupulous adherence to the code of behavior instilled by one's parents. Memphis and the wider world offered a host of enticements that could be negotiated only with care.

Given the amount of commentary about "licentious Negroes" in the journals of the 1880s, and given some of the "humorous" messages emblazoned on newly popular trade cards, it was perhaps not surprising that one Memphis reporter felt it necessary, in profiling the wedding of the well-to-do Robert R. Church, to explain to white readers that not all blacks were degraded. Still, the article felt a little as if it had pulsed down the telegraph lines from another planet. "There is as much distinction in the society of colored people of the South," the journalist declared, "as there is among the whites. In every community, town and city the blacks are divided into classes governed by education, intelligence, morality, wealth and respectability. This distinction is scrupulously observed here in Memphis by the colored people. The educated and intelligent who, by honest

Brightly hued trade cards became a popular way to sell products during the 1880s and 1890s. They trafficked in stereotypes, although the exaggerations usually moved in opposite directions, according to the race being portrayed.

industry, have accumulated a competency and who live exemplary lives create a fashionable social circle of their own."[4]

In the chase for respectability, Wells proved no different from millions of Americans, black or white. As a schoolteacher she received a salary ample enough to enjoy—with scrimping and saving—the store-bought goods being turned out in an increasingly industrialized America. Fancy butter dishes and pepperboxes (not merely for herself but also as wedding and Christmas gifts), parasols, handkerchiefs, seersucker and silk fabrics, gloves, jewelry, photograph and autograph albums to preserve memories, a whisk broom to keep everything tidy—she used all these items and more.[5] On Ida's twenty-fifth birthday, her heart filled "with thankfulness to My Heavenly Father for His wonderful love & kindness; for His bountiful goodness to me, that He has not caused me to want, & that I have always been provided with the means to make an honest livelihood."

Material goods were pleasing, but Wells's hunger for intellectual pursuits proved stronger. As she meditated on the course of her life, she noted, "Excepting my regret that I am not so good a Christian as the goodness of my Father demands, there is nothing for which I lament the wasted opportunities as I do my neglect to pick up the crumbs of knowledge that were within my reach."[6] The regrets arose only because she held herself to high standards. Wells read newspapers and journals as well as poetry and genteel novels, including those by former Confederate author Augusta Evans. Even on Easter Sunday she found time to begin *She* by Rider Haggard, the splashy, trashy adventure novel about a mysterious white goddess who ruled an underground kingdom in Africa. (Wells was curious to discover why the book was "creating such a stir.")[7]

The life of the mind was social as well as solitary. At evening soirées, young women of talent were regularly called upon to recite, sing, or play. Less formally Ida and her friends organized "entertainments"—dances or semiformal parties. And then there were places like the Golden Star Club, where a band might serenade but the call also went up for volunteers to entertain the crowd. A resourceful performer had more than one piece in her repertoire, appropriate for different occasions. One night at the Golden Star, Ida chose a humorous piece of dialect to recite, "The Widder Bud" ("The Widow Bud"), but for more elevated occasions she fancied "The Doom of Claudius and Cynthia," about star-crossed lovers facing the lions at the Roman Coliseum.[8] Many performance pieces were popular standbys. Ida heard more than one rendition of "'Ostler Joe," a heart-wrenching poem about a London swell who steals a foolish wife from her devoted, humble husband:

> I stood at eve, as the sun went down, by a grave where a woman lies,
> Who lured men's souls to the shores of sin with the light of her wanton eyes;
> Who sang the song that the Siren sang on the treacherous Lurley height,
> Whose face was as fair as a summer day, and whose heart was as black as night.[9]

To acquit herself creditably (and with an eye to a possible acting career), Wells took elocution lessons with a fellow schoolteacher, Mrs. Fannie Thompson. The price of fifty cents a lesson was difficult to meet, and sometimes Ida had to do without. But she kept at it, usually on Saturday mornings. For one recitation

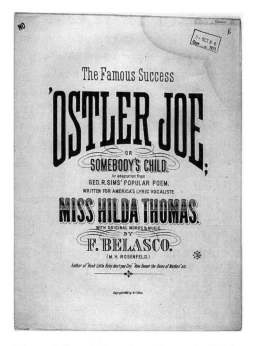

Often recited, songwriters also set the popular "'Ostler Joe" to music.

performed with a fellow teacher, the two donned period costumes to render a dialogue between Queen Elizabeth and her archrival Mary Queen of Scots. A newspaper correspondent hailed the delivery as the "crowning literary effort of the evening."[10]

As her reputation spread, both as teacher and performer, Wells came to the attention of Julia Britton Hooks, one of the city's leading black teachers and a musician since the age of five. Mrs. Hooks invited Wells to one of her concerts in June 1886. The honor was significant. Hooks was Ida's senior by ten years and her soirées were events of note in Memphis. Quick-witted as well as learned, Hooks prevented a panic once when a blocked chimney flue set her schoolhouse to burning. At the concert Ida recited "The Letter Reading," for which she was "loudly applauded." Then she donned a loose Mother Hubbard dress, commonly worn by pregnant women, which served for a nightgown as she portrayed Shakespeare's sleepwalking Lady Macbeth, hands seemingly stained by the blood of those she had helped to murder. "Out, damned spot! out, I say!…What, will these hands ne'er be clean?—No more o' that, my lord, no more o' that: you mar all with this starting…Here's the smell of the blood still: all the perfumes of Arabia will not sweeten this little hand. Oh, oh, oh!" Ever critical, Ida felt that her performance was "not so effective as I could have wished."[11]

Wells shared with Julia Britton Hooks the determination to stand up for civil rights. When Tennessee began segregating theaters as well as rail lines, Hooks refused to sit in the newly established "colored" balcony of the Jefferson Theater. She found herself promptly arrested and carried out by two police officers. Just as white newspapers mocked Wells as a "darky damsel," they patronized Hooks as a "dusky damsel" and "a cheeky wench" out to make trouble. That she dressed respectably seemed actually to count as a demerit. One reporter smirked that she was "decorated in her best store clothes," not to mention "perfumed to the highest essence."[12]

The concerts were social high points of the year, but Ida enjoyed more ordinary evenings as well, when she gathered with like-minded teachers for the LeMoyne Literary Society, sponsored

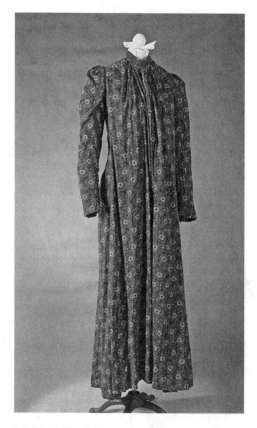

Mother Hubbard dress, ca. 1890s

by the local teachers' college, as well as the Memphis Lyceum, a group meeting Friday afternoons after school at the Vance Street Church. The programs included debates on current affairs, essays given by members, and the usual recitations interspersed by music.

The Lyceum published a newspaper, the *Evening Star,* featuring the group's essays and poetry along with letters and comments. Its editor, Virginia Broughton, was the woman who joined Ida in portraying Queen Elizabeth and Mary Queen of Scots.

A CHEEKY WENCH

Causes a Commotion in the Theater and is Locked Up Therefor.

A little civil rights commotion was kicked up at the Theater yesterday prior to the matinee performance by an irate dusky damsel, Julia Hooks, who claims to be a school-teacher. Julia was decorated in her best store clothes, and was perfumed to the highest essence. She crowded in between the white ladies and children who were purchasing tickets of admission at the box-office. The ticket-seller informed her that she must not do that, but must take her place in the line and come to the office-window in regular order. This she refused to do, and becoming excited until she became black as from coffee-colored, she abused the ticket-seller roundly. Patrolman Rogers, who was present, removed her, but this only excited her more. She shook her fist at him, and dared him to touch her. After acting in a most disgraceful and disorderly manner, she secured a ticket and rushed up stairs to the family circle, half of which is allotted to the whites and half to the blacks, and neither race is permitted to intrude in the portion of the circle devoted to the use of the other. When she got to the head of the stairs, she was directed to go on around to the place designated for and occupied by colored people. She apparently assented, saying, "I know where to go," and, turning suddenly, she darted down among the white people. She was immediately removed and ejected from the building while she gave utterance to violent language, and, when on the street, became so obstreperous, insulting and disorderly that the police arrested her and carried her to stationhouse, where she was locked up on a charge of disorderly conduct.

Mrs. Julia Britton Hooks and an article recounting her attempt to desegregate a Memphis theater, from the Memphis Daily Appeal, *March 13, 1881*

To close the afternoon's business, Broughton read from a regularly featured column in the *Evening Star,* involving news and notes about people in the community. Ida called it a "spicy journal"—no doubt because the notes possessed enough edge to make them interesting. People do want to know what's being said about each other, which is why gossip columns never go out of style. This one was titled "They Say."

They say:

> She is about four and half feet high, tolerably well proportioned, about twenty Summers, and of ready address. Her ambition is not found in most girls, or women either…(*Washington Bee,* 1885)[13]
>
> She is rather girlish looking in physique, with sharp regular features, penetrating eyes, firm set thin lips and a sweet voice…she is as smart as a steel trap, and she has no sympathy with humbug. (*New York Age,* 1888)[14]

So wrote two of Ida's male admirers—she had many. To find herself so well liked was a pleasant dilemma, for she enjoyed the company of men. There was the natural attraction of the opposite sex, of course. But Ida also relished male friendship because she could speak of more than the usual home-bound topics thought proper to a women's world. She enjoyed intellectual discussions and wished to be taken seriously. She took pleasure in competing on a level field and winning. ("We had an interesting game of checkers, in which I beat—of course surprising him greatly," she noted of one suitor.[15]) The dilemma was that men took her very seriously. At least a dozen admirers were smitten by her engaging air, astonished by her talents and—to their great chagrin—driven utterly to distraction when she would not fall at their feet as a conquest. Many of these men were not shy about pressing their advantage. They called on her at home, escorted her to church, wrote fervent letters, bestowed photographs of themselves in return for hers, went on walks, sought *opportunities*.

All the more reason, then, to insist on the proprieties. Going to a meeting or party unescorted was out of the question; it would send the wrong signal about her availability. "Was to have gone to LeMoyne last night…but I had no one to go with," she wrote one evening. On another Ida wrote, "Expected to attend a party given last week but my escort did not come."[16] Even if she ran into someone in the street whom she recognized but had not met, decorum prevented her from speaking. She caught sight of the editor of the *Little Rock Sun* in a train depot once, "but as [our mutual acquaintance] Mr. Hall did not come to the train with me I did not get an introduction to him."[17]

On the other hand, a young man who had made a formal acquaintance was free to begin calling. "Was introduced to Messrs Forbes & Hibbler—the former went home with me, the latter called next day but I was not at home." On another occasion she noted, "I had 4 callers tonight who came in simultaneously and remained the same length of time." Yet another day she "strolled home to find that I had had a caller but an unknown one, as he left no card and no one could tell who it was."[18]

Letters sometimes provided a more intimate ground than face-to-face encounters. The handwritten word could both reveal and hide; expose feelings while maintaining distance. In a world in which the telephone was yet an exotic novelty, letters were a mainstay of communication. They were a daily part of Ida's life and bound her not only to friends in distant cities and states but also across town—or occasionally even next door, in cases where a letter made things easier to say:

> Mr. Lawson came to the door and handed me a note. Little thinking of the contents I toyed carelessly with it—but on my utter surprise when opening it, I found it to be a notification that I had circulated the report that he wearied me with his attentions! He wrote to beg pardon for the one offence of having asked my company once[,] assuring me it would not happen again. I was very angry and shocked; I racked my brain trying to remember anything I might have said that could be so construed but could not—and wrote & told him so & repeated what I had said.[19]

Poor Lawson! He continued to write from time to time and Wells answered, but never with particular interest.

She kept a portable writing desk with a locked compartment for correspondence, receiving or sending as many as seven letters a day. Once she did "10 letters at a stretch."[20] She remembered the dates when her notes went out; knew how long it would take each to reach its destination and therefore, how long it should take to receive a prompt reply. For friends who lagged, especially if she were eager to hear from them, she let them know her disappointment. "I answered two days later & told him my delay was intentional & why it was so." If the reply returned early, so much the better. "Found a letter from Mr. C. S. M. on my arrival home this afternoon instead of tomorrow as I expected."[21]

"C. S. M." was Mr. Charles S. Morris, a journalist from Louisville, Kentucky, with whom Ida began corresponding in 1885. She warmed to him immediately. His letters were "bright, enthusiastic, and witty" and he had a self-deprecating sense of humor, not least about the scrawl that passed for penmanship. "Read what you can," he warned, "& guess at the rest." The letters were always "couched in such chaste and apt language I am instructed entertained and amused," she noted. "His fine humor & sarcasm are very refreshing."[22] Mr. Morris had literary ambitions. Recognizing Ida's abilities with a pen he proposed that the two of them collaborate on a novel. The notion caused her "to smile in derision of myself at daring to dream of such a thing—but his enthusiasm is catching." They wrote back and forth with ideas, but the most detailed plot he sketched seemed "rather sensational." Still, Mr. Morris was clearly "what I have long wished for as a correspondent, an interested, intellectual being who could lead & direct my wavering footsteps in intellectual paths."[23]

Any romantic notions hit a bump, however, upon receipt of his photograph. "I told him I liked the face," she said, but was in fact shocked by what she saw. "It is the face of a mere boy; whereas I had been led, from his writings to suppose him a man." He asked Wells for a word portrait of herself along with a photograph, but for Ida decorum suddenly intervened. She described herself without mentioning her age, "till I know his, as I wish to make the unpleasant discovery that I am his senior—first."[24] Still, Morris's letters were so diverting that within a few months she began to "hate the barren formality of our address to each other." She wanted to begin "My dear Charlie" rather than "Dear Mr. Morris," but she hesitated "about breaking the ice, tho' I know the advance ought and must come from me."[25] Even when the ice was broken, in her diary Ida could not help placing "Charlie" between quotation marks. As their friendship deepened, she began calling him "Charlie boy" and finally even, in deference to the Southern lilt, "Challie boy."[26] Yet for all his wisdom, Charlie *boy* remained very much a youth in Ida's eyes.

The exchange of photographs often proved vexing. Even the act of sending one implied a certain bond of intimacy. Custom demanded that one keep a supply in stock, but even the cheapest "carte de visites" cost over a dollar a dozen. "Cabinets"—larger portraits about four inches by six—retailed at $2.50 the dozen and up.[27] Ida doled them out with infinite care, allowing only her closest friends to keep them. The rest were on loan. To Charlie she mailed "two different pictures to look at—so he might not forget me, but they are to be returned." Half grudgingly, she complained when another new acquaintance "wheedled" a photograph out of her; and she positively bridled when her landlady gave one to a visitor without permission, while she was away. Even less fortunate was a young physician, Dr. Sidney Burchett, who may have been a former admirer. While leafing through Burchett's album the night of his wedding celebration, Ida encountered one of her portraits loaned some time earlier. "I took the picture I loaned Dr. B from his album…he says I did so because I was jealous of he and S [presumably the new bride]. I gave him a piece of my mind concerning so untruthful & ungentlemanly a trick & he denied it every bit. The soft cake!"[28]

Inevitably questions of romance intruded into the workplace. There she encountered the admiration of Mr. I. J. Graham, a fellow teacher. Graham was ambitious, young, hardworking, and thrifty to boot. In later years he gained the reputation of being the wealthiest teacher in Tennessee. Such practical virtues gained him nothing, however, in the game of love. Ida's beauty and candor rendered him by turns tongue-tied or excessively playful, bringing down the wrath of the lady he admired. The result was an awkward two-step of a courtship in which Graham regularly overreached himself and was forced to retreat and sorely repent. Teasing Ida one evening in the rain, he snatched her hat and made off with it, forcing her to walk home bareheaded. She took the jest "all in good part till I saw my hat next morning & then I became very angry for it was utterly ruined." She refused to speak to him for two days.[29]

There must have been something redeeming about the man, for she refused to dismiss him. Yet every time he came to visit he appeared to wilt before her formidable presence. It felt like standing around in too tight a jacket, he remarked. "Mr. G came out and sat like a mummy for some time & left with little benefit from his visit," she noted. On another occasion, when Ida was "very blue" all day, he came by "trying to comfort me but he makes a mess of it always." Clearly he was in love—but if so, why not declare his feelings outright, instead of hinting? "He renewed his question of a former occasion as if I would tell him I 'cared for him' without a like assertion on his part. He seems to think I ought to encourage him to speak by speaking first—but that I'll never do. It's conceding too much and I don't think I need buy any man's love. I blush to think I allowed him to caress me, that he would dare take such liberties and yet not make a declaration."[30]

While Mr. Graham puzzled over how to proceed, a rival of strikingly different temperament launched a flanking attack. Where Graham was precise and awkward, Mr. Louis M. Brown was self-assured and well traveled: a Memphis man who, in 1886, worked for the *Washington Bee,* a black paper in the nation's capital. In correspondence he easily surmounted the formality of being addressed as "Mr. Brown" by adopting the French mode of "ma chere amie," to which Ida willingly replied with "mon ami" or "ma chere frere." Still, such sophistication repelled as well as attracted a woman for whom moral respectability was paramount. Mr. Brown thought himself "a blasé man of the world," Ida judged, "with no new worlds to conquer or nothing fresh or new to be, for him, learned under the sun." Like Graham, Brown would sometimes point out her faults, and she would fire back in high dudgeon. "I gave him my candid opinion of his petty mode of warfare," she reported—though without breaking off the relationship, for in the next breath she asked if he would purchase for her a copy of "Guttmann's Aesthetic Physical Self-Culture," for which she promised to reimburse him.[31]

Brown kept her off balance. One moment they were in a state of "petty warfare," in the next, he declared his affections—with the insinuating remark added, "I could understand you better in another way." In March 1886, he reported that he had been fired by the *Washington Bee* (received the "grand bounce" was the way he put it) and was returning to Memphis. Ida wrote immediately, saying she "would be glad to see him," but Brown fell unaccountably silent for some weeks. Nearly as suddenly he "arrived on the scene" looking as handsome as ever "and I was real glad to see him," Ida enthused—so much so, that she skipped an evening of tutoring to go walking.

It was spring: the flowers in bloom, the air full of life. Brown began to meet Ida at school and walk her home. Evenings, he called regularly for long walks and talks. Once they strolled all the way to the home of an acquaintance near the edge of the city, "& when we returned the moon was shining so clear, calm and bright that we sat in the moonlight and enjoyed the scene. It was delightful. The din, dust and smoke seemed left far behind; all was peaceful calm and still; the mellow moonlight air was beautiful and the landscape spread out before us." Then—after walking her home from the afternoon Easter service at Avery Chapel—Brown dropped from sight. "Have seen nothing of L.M.B. for nearly two weeks," she reported, annoyed enough that when he returned in mid-May to join an outing with a number of friends, she "hardly noticed" him.

The neglect may also have reflected the renewed energy of Mr. Graham. At an entertainment Ida attended, Graham was struck by her beauty. Ida looked radiant in a black silk dress set off by diamonds (the jewelry borrowed from a friend). She was anxious because the festivities included a quadrille, which she had never danced; but after taking a successful turn or two, bowing and sashaying, she began to enjoy herself "hugely." Mr. Marcus, another admirer, "attempted familiarity" but she quickly rebuffed him. Mr. Dardis asked if she wouldn't read a dramatic piece for his concert, to be held the following week, and she thought she would. The present evening's entertainment had required a contribution of $1.50—a real strain on her budget—and if she performed for Mr. Dardis, the fee for his party would be waived.

In the midst of this excitement, Graham seized the moment. If he couldn't bring himself to tell her directly that he loved her, a bit of poetry might turn the trick. On a slip of paper he presented some verse that indicated he knew she cared for him, concluding,

I long to sip
the nectar from your curling lip.[32]

Ida read the lines, a little flustered at receiving the note on such a public occasion. Etiquette suggested returning the offering if the sentiments were unwelcome. Did she love him? Louis Brown seemed to have deserted her. Then too, only the week before she had returned a batch of letters from Mr. B. F. Poole, another admirer. Despite the rejection, Poole wrote back declaring her "the twin mate of his soul," and Ida was so unsure now of her own feelings, she thought he might be "telling the truth." On the other hand, Mr. Graham was earnest—and determined. She read his note in silence, but did not return it.

That was encouragement enough. Tuesday evening Graham came to call and stayed until Ida's chaperone and landlord, Mr. Settle, finally retired. Then he asked her to kiss him. Ida wanted a declaration of love first, if not a proposal. "Another lost opportunity of his, for springing the question that evidently seems uppermost in his mind."[33]

The concluding school year blocked any immediate advances. All of the exams, recitations, and celebrations left Ida "tired out—as we have been on the pad, night & day, for nearly two weeks."[34] But once school was out, Graham made another visit and, this time, called her bluff. He loved her, he said; did she love him too? The tactic of silence, which had sometimes stood Ida in good stead, was no longer a refuge.

She surely didn't want to disappoint him or reject out of hand a respectable suitor. But did she love him—truly? Yes, she replied, but then added more honestly that she was not conscious of an "absorbing" feeling. And Louis Brown was back in town and called the next day. Graham's rival took Ida on yet another long walk. He had a "trysting spot" to which he liked to retire—something that always made her uneasy, for he was inclined there to press his luck. To her surprise he spoke more loftily about the goals she should pursue and less of his own narrow interests, which gave her "a higher opinion of himself than I've had."

For most of June the two vied for her time and affections, with Brown impressing her more. One cozy evening during a pouring rain he confessed that he had actually been engaged for a time to a girl in Georgia. (Could this have explained his sudden disappearances from time to time?) Instead of becoming jealous, Ida admired his frankness. That same afternoon she was escorted home by the Reverend A. A. Mosely, yet another admirer who was paying compliments. "With me, my affairs are always at one extreme or the other," she wrote. "I either have an abundance of company or none at all. Just now there are three in the city who, with the least encouragement, would make love to me; I have two correspondents in the same predicament—but past experience will serve to keep me from driving them from me. I am enjoying existence very much just now; I don't wonder longer, but will enjoy life as it comes. I am an anomaly to my self as well as to others. I do not wish to be married but I do wish for the society of the gentlemen."[35]

With so many men competing for her attention, was it chance only that she accepted an invitation from an older friend in Woodstock to leave town for a week? Her primary suitors reacted each in characteristic fashion. Graham stopped by to say farewell while she was away on errands and never returned to say his goodbyes. ("I must be loved with more warmth than that," she huffed.) Brown, whether consciously or not, employed reverse psychology, writing a letter while she was away in which he told her he almost dreaded the influence she was having on him, "as he was afraid he was falling in love." He begged her to return to Memphis. Yet in the next breath he announced he was leaving for Washington, D.C.

Instantly Ida replied with her own mixed message. She "believed him incapable of love in its strongest, best sense," she asserted, and then earnestly advised him not to depart for Washington because she would return Saturday night as he requested.

Brown sensed his chance. The attraction of this vibrant twenty-four-year-old woman—so bold, intelligent, energetic—so damnably hard to get—propelled him to action:

> Mr. B came out and persuaded me to go walking with him & he forced me to our trysting place. I weakly yielded to his importunities to be seated and then he too told me a tale of love and asked me directly if I were pledged to any one. I could not say yea, and I did say nay. For with all the encouragement I've given G he has not sought to bind me to him & seems so utterly indifferent that I don't and can't feel that I belong to him. I told Mr. B I did not love him, but I was sorry that would cause a cessation of his visits. He talked sometime longer and then begged so hard for the right to pay his addresses to me to hope, that I could not satisfactorily give. But he kissed me—twice—& it seems even now as if they blistered my lips. I feel so humiliated in my own estimation at the thought that I cannot look any one straight in the face. I feel somehow as if I were defrauded of something since then.[36]

That night she lay in bed, the scene burned in memory. She thought of her landlord, Mr. Settle, who had patiently watched a succession of young men come calling. She knew he could not understand why she did not just find someone who would make her happy and marry him. Why did she lead on first one suitor, then another? Everyone told her she was heartless, incapable of love: Louis Brown, the Reverend Moseley. "You are playing with edged tools," Mr. Settle had warned this morning over the breakfast table. Why did men find it impossible to enjoy her society without thinking they must make love to her, let alone pursue her hand in marriage?

"God helping me," she prayed, "I will free myself from this predicament, somehow…"[37]

· *Five* ·

AMBITION TO EDIT

❧—❦

IN THE MIDST OF HER CONFLICTS OVER MEN AND MARRIAGE, AN
escape presented itself. The seeming way out of her dilemma
came from the woman who had invited Ida to Memphis in the
first place, Aunt Fannie Butler.

In January 1886, Butler moved to Visalia, California, a small
town in the San Joaquin Valley. She had taken along Ida's younger
sisters, Annie and Lily (then roughly twelve and nine years old),
with the understanding that Ida would follow as soon as circumstances permitted. Fanny had three children of her own, including a daughter named Ida about Annie's age. That spring Wells
sent money out whenever she could, often feeling guilty for not
sending more.

As school let out and summer ripened, a succession of letters
and then telegrams arrived from Visalia, each more insistent, urging
Ida to come out and take the teachers' qualifying exam. With her
life so full, she delayed, put off, postponed, made excuses. Her
railroad suit appeared on the brink of settlement, and she was
being invited to perform at the concert given by Mrs. Julia Britton
Hooks. More to the point, two suitors seemed on the verge of

proposing. By late June, however, with neither I. J. Graham nor Louis Brown making her feel comfortable about the prospect of marriage, she wrote Aunt Fannie that she was coming. As a bonus, she could stop on the way in Kansas City to attend a national teachers' convention. In any case, the supreme court of Tennessee had put off her railroad suit for yet another term.[1]

The convention was great fun. There were "crowds and crowds of people! I never saw so many teachers in my life." In Colorado, Ida drank from mountain springs but passed up a chance to climb Pike's Peak—she lacked the warm clothes and sturdy shoes needed. In Salt Lake City she visited the Mormon Tabernacle where she "listened to a harangue" given by one of the church elders. In San Francisco she toured the crowded streets of Chinatown where she saw "thousands of 'Heathen Chinee' in all branches of industry" and marveled at the fog-shrouded Pacific, where the seals lined the rocky beaches "like so many brown bags."[2]

When Wells arrived at last in Visalia she found a hot, dusty, cheerless village of a few thousand souls. It took only week before she was devouring every letter from home and feeling "so far away from everything & everybody."

Why on earth had Aunt Fannie chosen the spot? The town had been founded by Kentucky slave owners and its present white inhabitants were former Confederate sympathizers. The one-room school where Ida would teach was dusty, ramshackle, and segregated. Whites used the more spacious facilities on the hill—as did the Mexican and Indian children. The blacks seemed resigned to their situation. They actually had *asked* for separate facilities.[3]

Was this the kind of life a generation of free African Americans should be accepting? Ida did not so much voice the question as live her way through to an answer. Despite the complications of Memphis, the city provided so much more in the way of possibilities. Visalia offered "no books, no companionship." When a male acquaintance from San Francisco came up for a visit, the time slipped by so deliciously that she hated to see him go "& started down to the depot" to see him off. "But it was so hot & dusty & the people stared so, I gave it up & bade him goodby at the post office."[4]

Aunt Fannie insisted that Ida's duty lay with her family. But in the tug of war between duty and a life with possibilities, Memphis won out, even though the train fare home had to be borrowed. By the end of September Ida was on her way, taking Lily with her and allowing Annie to stay with her cousin Ida, with whom she was close. Homeward bound, Wells was "jubilant with the idea of soon meeting friends." Almost miraculously her romantic entanglements vanished. The peripatetic Louis Brown had moved to Kansas City to work for the *Gate City Press,* where he tried unsuccessfully to persuade her to remain when she passed through. I. J. Graham, after one unproductive visit to welcome her home, became convinced she had lost her heart to another man. Within a few weeks, he abruptly married someone else.[5]

With or without the entanglements, Ida recognized that living in California made no sense. Over the past three years in Memphis, she had not only established a full social life, she was moving slowly but steadily away from the profession of teaching and toward journalism. What spurred this move were the railroad cases. When Wells first sued the C&O in the winter of 1883–1884, Memphis minister Robert N. Countee was in the process of launching a black newspaper, the *Living Way.* Perhaps he had met Ida at church; almost certainly he made his way one

Friday afternoon to the Memphis Lyceum, where teachers took turns reading their essays. Countee asked Wells to write about her railroad experience and she agreed—without pay, of course, for the weekly was operating on the usual lean budget.[6] The article was well received, so Countee solicited others.

The opportunity to be published was gratifying, if only a small step up from Wells's occasional essays for the Memphis Lyceum. What made the crucial difference was that Countee sent the *Living Way* to a number of nonlocal subscribers, including T. Thomas Fortune, a sharp-eyed editor of another black paper, the *New York Globe*. The *Globe* called attention to Wells's railroad article in May 1884.

When Ida finally had a chance to see a portrait of the man who discovered her, she was disappointed. "With his long hair, curling about his forehead and his spectacles he looks more like the dude of the period than the strong, sensible, brainy man I have pictured him—But then, as I told Charlie M[orris], one should not judge a person by the cut or rather uncut of his hair any more than by his clothes." She was right not to, for Fortune recognized Wells's talents. In January 1885, he ran a story on the second railroad suit. The following month he printed an essay of hers on a completely different subject, politics.[7] It was not long before word spread of the young female journalist with a pungent pen.

The attention came thanks to the network of black journalists and newspapers in both the North and South. In the two decades following emancipation, dozens of black newspapers had sprung up. They were determined to deliver news long neglected or distorted by the mainstream press. These weeklies searched eagerly for subscribers and advertisers, benefited by the support of religious organizations and buoyed in the 1880s by a growing black

T. THOMAS FORTUNE.

T. Thomas Fortune

urban middle class. Even so, the going was difficult. Although more than eighteen hundred different black newspapers were published across the country before 1915, few lasted more than a year or two.[8] Some managed to publish only one issue before giving up. Many more published erratically at best. Often they were one-person or family operations begun in one town and then moved, with their owners, to another, to reappear under new names. "Colored newspapers are monuments to self-sacrifice, devotion, industry and energy" observed the *Indianapolis Freeman;* "the chances for making money are—none."[9] Fortune's *New York Globe* (later renamed the *Freeman* and after that the *Age)* was one of the best known, but there were others that were reasonably well established: the *Washington Bee,* the *Detroit Plaindealer,* the *Cleveland Gazette,* the *Richmond Planet,* and the *Indianapolis Freeman,* not to mention church publications like the *Living Way* and the *American Baptist.*

The networks forged by such papers linked editors, writers, and subscribers. Newspapers excerpted one another and readers passed clippings from one friend to the next. "I answered & returned Mr. D's letter," noted Wells, "and sent him Miss Gaines' article, my answer and The Fisk Herald article to read."[10] The editors and writers of these papers, being a peripatetic lot, often knew each other personally from moving about, just as Louis Brown had jumped from the *Washington Bee* to the *Gate City Press* in Kansas City. Umbrella organizations like the National Colored Press Association held conventions where journalists mixed, met, and delivered talks. The papers feuded constantly. "Honey for friends; stings for enemies," promised the *Washington Bee,* while the Republican-oriented *Cleveland Gazette* attacked the politically independent Thomas Fortune as "the merest lickspittle."[11] Almost immediately Wells was drawn into this network as journalists wrote her in response to her essays. In his early attempts to correspond with her, Charlie Morris sent a letter care of the *Living Way,* where Wells's railroad articles had first appeared. Wells asked Louis Brown to send Morris an issue of the *Washington Bee,* which may have contained an item about her. Her mention in Fortune's *New York Globe* no doubt attracted the attention of another New York journalist, J. A. Arneaux, who began corresponding.[12]

Most members of this free-speaking, free-swinging guild were male, but women journalists were hardly unknown. Gertrude Mossell of Philadelphia became well respected in the 1880s, wrote for many black newspapers including Thomas Fortune's *Freeman,* and eventually for the white press as well. By 1886, she was earning $500 a year, double the average income of a white woman working in Pennsylvania. Wells's older Memphis friend Julia Britton Hooks had a younger sister Mary, or "Meb," who wrote for a newspaper in Lexington, Kentucky.[13] The great majority of female journalists, however, stuck to topics meant to appeal to others of their sex. Wells covered such subjects too, including essays on "Women's Mission" and "The Model Woman."[14] Yet because her first article discussed railroad segregation, she could lay claim to discussing "politics and other matters of national importance with the vivacity of a full-fledged journalist of the masculine gender," as the *Cleveland Gazette* put it.[15]

Wells entered eagerly into this spirited dialogue of ambition and eloquence, protest and petty bickering as African American journalists sought to define what it meant to be black and free. A wide variety of news, large and small, was worthy of publication. If "an Omaha clothing house employ[ed] a colored salesman," that was news. So was the ejection of the black physician D. W. Culp from his position at the hospital in Augusta, Georgia; or the performance of Charles Winter Wood, a black actor playing the part of Richard III in Chicago. When Charleston was hit by an earthquake in 1886, African Americans there solicited aid from other cities.

Larger debates raged constantly. How should one deal with the increasing segregation on trains? Did it make sense to participate fully in white society, or would blacks progress faster by separating themselves? How could teachers contribute to the uplifting of the African race?[16] Wells spoke out forcefully on many such issues. Early on, she attacked the traditional notion that the Republican Party

The masthead of the Indianapolis Freeman

deserved the unwavering support of blacks. Stay independent, she counseled; weigh carefully how each party might advance black interests. Perhaps because she was treading controversial ground—or more likely because it was a common literary custom—she began signing her essays with a pen name, "Iola."[17]

Writing on such topics, Wells remained independent, stubborn, insistent. After all, her father had been a "race man" and proud of it; so was she. When she filed her railroad suit, she had been surprised how few friends rallied around. It was not that they opposed her; they just didn't seem to feel that the litigation was a particular concern of theirs. When she traveled to the teachers' convention in Kansas City, her friends wanted to try out the new sleeper cars on the C&O line. Ida protested that she was "unable and unwilling to do so" and preferred to take "the regular KC route."[18] Furthermore, many well-to-do African Americans seemed unwilling to speak out against separate car laws. "They are able to pay for berths and seats in Pullman cars, and consequently can report that—'railroad officials don't bother me, in traveling,'" she complained.[19]

Black business folk in the service trades had economic reasons for not pushing hard against the increasingly sharp lines of segregation that were being drawn. A barber who earned his living giving haircuts and shaves to whites understood that many would resent black customers sitting in the same chairs. Methodist bishop Henry McNeal Turner reassured whites that he preferred segregated accommodations. "I don't find much trouble in traveling at the south on account of my color, for the simple reason that I am not in the habit of pushing myself where I am not wanted," he noted.[20] Wells admired Turner but could not agree. If blacks accepted separation or, worse, promoted it as a positive good, the situation would only deteriorate, she argued:

> We howl about the discrimination exercised by other races, unmindful that we are guilty of the same thing. The spirit that keeps Negroes out of the colleges and places him by himself, is the same that drives him into the smoking car; the spirit that makes colored men run excursions with "a separate car for our white friends," etc. provides separate seats for them when they visit our concerts, exhibitions, etc. is the same that sends the Negro to theatre and church galleries and second-class waiting rooms; the feeling that prompts colored barbers, hotel keepers and the like to refuse accommodation to their own color is the momentum that sends a Negro right about when he presents himself at any similar first-class establishment run by white men.[21]

At first Wells received no money for her work, but when the *Gate City Press* requested an article in January 1886, she asked the editor if he would pay. "State your price," came the reply and she was inexperienced enough to find the question embarrassing. "I have no idea of its worth & shall tell him so." Two months later when the *Detroit Plaindealer* inquired, she was ready to ask $2 per article, but that was beyond the newspaper's reach, or "so they say," she noted in her diary.[22] Still, she wrote for the *Gate City* and the *Plaindealer*—and promptly hinted in another essay that journalists deserved better pay. This led the editor at the *Washington Bee* to sting Iola—he called her the "star-eyed goddess" whose "trenchant pen" was producing entirely enough verbiage, with or without pay.[23]

The generally positive reception, however, served to whet Wells's ambition. She used her diary to record material for future articles, including a sidewalk conflict of the sort that perennially roiled race relations:

> It seems that a white and colored girl had been in the habit of passing and repassing, morning and evening, on a narrow path in the woods up the country, and there had never been manifested on the part of the white girl any desire to give half of the walk. One day they passed while the white girl's brother was with her and he pushed the girl from the path and abused her. The next day they met again when each were alone and the white girl attempted to imitate the example of her brother of the day previous and they fought; the colored girl getting the best of the fight, and she was reported.

The judge in the case ordered her sent to the workhouse for nearly a year.

Wells also recorded the case of a white man prevented from getting "a license to marry a colored girl" because of the laws against racial intermarriage. "He cut open her three fingers & sucked her blood & then told them he had negro blood in his veins & therewith procured a license." The man's friends, wishing to save him from what they considered a horrendous mistake, exposed the deception and proved that the groom's parents were Caucasian.[24]

Not long after returning from California, Wells was sought out by the Reverend William J. Simmons, a "lively & jolly" big-framed man who edited the *American Baptist*. The National Colored Press

Association was holding a convention the following summer in his hometown, Louisville, Kentucky. If Wells would supply him with essays on a regular basis, he would pay her way to the convention. Eventually he also agreed to pay a dollar for each article.[25]

The convention marked Wells's coming out as a figure of journalistic note. In Louisville she was swept up into one meeting after another, introduced at dinners and asked to speak impromptu. She visited the Colored Orphan House and took a moonlight excursion up the Ohio River. Halfway through her stay she ventured on a side trip to Lexington. All the while a stream of visitors stopped by her lodgings to pay their respects. "Had any number of callers last Sabbath, many of whose names I can't remember," she noted. Those she could remember included "Messrs Perry, Nixon, Childress, Upshaw, Bennett, McKinley, & Minor." So many others left their cards that she began to think "half Louisville had been to call."[26]

A reporter from New Orleans captured the reaction of many. Iola was "brilliant and earnest…the most prominent correspondent at present connected with the Negro press. If she does not suffer her head to become unduly inflated, there is a brilliant and useful future opening before her."[27] Another female journalist who came, Lucy Wilmot Smith, confirmed Wells's status in an appreciation written two years later:

> Miss Ida B. Wells, "Iola," has been called the "Princess of the Press," and she has well earned the title. No writer, the male fraternity not excepted, has been more extensively quoted; none struck harder blows at the wrongs and weaknesses of the race. Her readers are equally divided between the sexes. She reaches the men by dealing with the political aspect of the race questions, and the women she meets around the fireside…

By the way it is her ambition to edit a paper. She believes there is no agency so potent as the press in reaching and elevating a people.[28]

❧—✦

Why not take the helm of a newspaper? The previous October Wells had been elected "editress" of the *Evening Star,* the amateur journal put out by the Lyceum. Several other black publications were making their way in Memphis. In addition to the *Living Way*, Wells wrote occasionally for the *Watchman* and the *Free Speech*, the latter recently launched by the Reverend Taylor Nightingale, the new pastor of Beale Street Baptist, as well as for the *Marion Headlight,* which was published just across the river in Arkansas.

White newspapers never hired Wells, although they printed her letters from time to time. Their willingness to do so reflected the calmer race relations prevailing earlier in the decade. The owner of the *Memphis Avalanche,* James Phelan, echoed the views of those promoting a "New South," by insisting it was only proper to "accept in good part and in good faith the citizenship of the negro race. They are our fellow-Tennesseans. Their rights are as sacred as ours," even though "socially God has placed a wide and running river between us."[29]

In particular, the circumstances of Memphis city government allowed African Americans a more active role than in many areas of the South. The yellow fever epidemic of 1878, coming on the heels of a decade of financial speculation and graft, left the city bankrupt. The state set up a three-member commission to govern and, in the process, to reform the city's finances. Although the commission was appointed, its president was popularly elected. David P. Hadden, who assumed the office, courted the black vote, placed an African American on the board of public works, allowed black policemen onto the Memphis force, and did not object to blacks being elected to the school board.[30] "Pap" Hadden's moderate regime was one reason Wells remained a political independent.

Toward the end of the decade, however, Wells witnessed a worsening of relations between whites and blacks, not only in Memphis but across the South. One telltale came in April 1887 when at last the Tennessee Supreme Court ruled on her railroad suit. It overturned the lower court ruling despite clear evidence that Wells had been asked to ride in a car where smoking and drinking were permitted. The segregated car provided facilities equal "in every respect as to comfort, convenience, and safety," the court insisted. It accused Wells of being an agitator who had complained only "to harass with a view to this suit, and that her persistence was not in good faith to obtain a comfortable seat for the short ride."[31]

Ida was devastated.

> I felt so disappointed, because I had hoped such great things from my suit for my people generally. I have firmly believed all along that the law was on our side and would, when we appealed to it, give us justice. I feel shorn of that belief and utterly discouraged, and just now if it were possible would gather my race in my arms and fly far away with them. O God is there no redress, no peace, no justice in this land for us? Thou hast always fought the battles of the weak & oppressed. Come to my aid at this moment & teach me what to do, for I am sorely, bitterly disappointed.[32]

But the decade-long march toward segregation continued. In 1888, the single remaining black member of the Memphis board of education went down to defeat. For years, many middle- and upper-class whites had supported black education, as preparation for citizenship and for the factory and semiskilled jobs that advocates of the New South hoped would spread as the region embraced the industrial age. Increasingly, skeptics challenged that view. Educated African Americans had lost "a certain childish unconscious freedom of manner," complained one white newspaper, "and the insidious gnawing of ambitions and aspirations begin to eat into their minds and canker their feelings."[33]

In the end, whether the arguments were over separate transportation, separate accommodations, or separate education, they invoked the horror of "social equality," a euphemism for interracial "mixing." No sensible white men wanted "their wives and daughters to mix up in the same car, board at the same hotel and attend the same theater with the negro," advised one newspaper. Another laid bare the deeper dread with a mocking suggestion that blacks were agitating for access not only to the ladies car but also "the sleeper." The *Memphis Avalanche* put it baldly. "Every kind of social intercourse is a step in the direction of breaking down the barriers of race—in other words towards miscegenation."[34]

To keep the forces of segregation at bay, Wells had always advocated political independence, to force white candidates to seek black support at the ballot box. The situation changed, however, as Democrats worked to make voting more difficult for poor Southerners, black and white. In the 1880s and 1890s, as the economy swung wildly from boom to bust and back again, ruling elites across the South came increasingly to fear an upheaval from below. Making voting more difficult for those at the bottom promised to keep those at the top where they believed they belonged.

It also helped to topple Republicans dependent on the black vote. Southern whites noted that many Northern and Midwestern states were adopting a system of voting known as the Australian ballot. Heralded as a reform, the procedure used secret ballots in place of party tickets with their identifying images—like the red-and-black Republican tiger once used in Marshall County. Election officials could no longer tell which way a citizen was voting. The reform, however, made balloting more difficult for illiterate citizens, for now they had to select candidates from a bare list of names.

By 1889, Tennessee Democrats managed to push through a secret ballot law, along with a rule that forbid anyone from helping voters mark their choices. A $2 poll tax was added as further discouragement. The elections of 1890 showed the result. Democrats swept to victory even in areas that had voted consistently Republican. The change in Memphis was particularly striking. Republicans won less than 10 percent of the vote they had received in the previous state election.[35]

Disturbing news extended beyond the voting booth. Reports from around the South found their way into the papers with increasing frequency:

> The daily papers bring notice this morning that 13 colored men were shot down in cold blood yesterday in Miss[issippi]—Carroll co[unty], I think. O, God when will these massacres cease…(Wells, *Diary*, March 18, 1886)
>
> The nine-year-old daughter of Samuel Carter, a well-to-do farmer of Rowan county, was outraged on the morning of January 21st by an unknown negro. Bob Genders, of the neighborhood, was suspected, and a number of farmers went to his cabin and hanged him to the beam above his door. Just as Genders was in the throes of death word was brought that not he but John Hooper was

guilty, and Genders was cut down. (*Memphis Weekly Public Ledger,* February 7, 1889)

Just imagine two half-grown boys holding a Negro girl five years old in the fire until her eyes are burned out. For no other reason but because she was a Negress! (*Cleveland Gazette,* June 22, 1889)

Will Lewis, a boy from Tullahoma, Tennessee, was hanged for being for being drunk and "sassy" to white folks. (Wells, personal records, 1891)[36]

What to do? A week after the Tennessee courts rejected her case, Wells attended a public meeting of the Negro Mutual Protective Association, created by Memphis churches and black fraternal organizations determined to speak out against mob law. She came away "very much enthused…The Negro is beginning to think for himself and find out that strength for his people and consequently for him is to be found only in unity."[37] The following month, her friend Thomas Fortune led the formation of a National Afro-American League to coordinate the actions of similar groups. Wells spoke out strongly in favor of national direction. If African Americans remained as "passive onlookers" they would deserve to be called a "race of cowards," she insisted.[38]

Clearly the Republican Party was not going to help. Senator Henry Cabot Lodge of Massachusetts had sponsored a bill allowing federal authorities to investigate the kind of election fraud that was disfranchising black voters, but in 1890 the bill died amidst the horse-trading Republicans needed to win support for higher tariffs. A measure providing funds for black schools in the South suffered a similar fate.[39]

Across the river from Memphis in Marion, Arkansas, Democrats refused to wait for election "reforms." A mob of a hundred whites marched through town during the summer of 1888, rounded up about thirty of the leading African Americans and sent them packing, including two ministers and J. L. Fleming, the editor of the *Marion Headlight.* Taylor Nightingale of the *Free Speech* offered Fleming refuge. The two newspapers combined as the *Free Speech and Headlight.*[40] Fleming was not the first editor to seek shelter in Memphis. Jesse C. Duke had long spoken up for black rights in Alabama. As editor of the *Montgomery Herald,* he was angered by a lynching in August 1887. The charge that a young black man had raped a white woman was bogus, Duke believed; the couple had been lovers. In an editorial he ignored the stern white taboo against admitting any possibility of "race mixing." "Why is it that white women attract negro men now more than in former days? There was a time when such a thing was unheard of. There is a secret to this thing, and we greatly suspect it is the growing appreciation of white Juliets for colored Romeos." The editorial appeared Saturday. White papers reprinted it Sunday. The mob met Monday. Duke fled town disguised as a woman, taking a train to Memphis, where he met Wells, among others, before eventually heading west to start another paper in Arkansas.[41]

Duke and Wells were not the only African Americans who perceived the hypocrisy of condemning sexual relationships between white women and black men when so many white men conducted their own interracial affairs. Tennessee law forbid them, but the statute was never enforced against white men. In June 1889, a group of Memphis blacks announced their intention to press for a grand jury to indict over fifty white citizens who had taken black mistresses.[42]

That same month, Taylor Nightingale and J. L. Fleming invited Wells to join the staff of the *Free Speech and Headlight.*

She agreed, but only on equal terms. The two of them sold her a one-third interest in the business; and with Wells as editor, the paper trumpeted her conviction that African Americans should not meekly settle for white domination. "The dailies of our city say that the whites must rule this country. But that is an expression without a thought…The old Southern voice that was once heard and made the Negroes jump and run like rats to their holes is 'shut up,' or might well be, for the Negro of today is not the same as Negroes were thirty years back. So it is no use to be talking about how Negroes ought to be kept at the bottom where God intended them to stay; the Negro is not intended to stay at the bottom."[43] Yet as racial tensions worsened around the South, Wells wondered whether African Americans recognized their peril. "Agitate and act until *something* is done," she exhorted several months later. "While we are resting on our oars, seemingly content with expressing our indignation by resolutions at the outrages that daily occur, others are presuming upon this inaction and encroaching more and more upon our rights—nay upon life itself."[44]

❖—❖

Upon life itself. Horrible as lynchings were, one grew almost to expect the newspaper reports from one small town or another. It was in her own life, however, that Wells discovered the difficulty of predicting the complications produced by a society that painted in black and white.

By the spring of 1891, Wells had been teaching for more than a decade, and along the way wrote eloquently of the need to nurture young minds.[45] In truth, the day-to-day routine often wore her down, especially given the conditions under which black teachers worked. Her classes crowded as many as seventy children into a dilapidated room with only the barest equipment. As yet another school year moved toward its end, Wells wrote an article for the *Free Speech* outlining the handicaps under which black schools labored. She was angered, as well, by the politics played by some members of the school board. Charges had been made that some of the newer black recruits "had little to recommend them save an illicit friendship with members of the school board," Wells recalled years later. "I was sure that such a condition deserved criticism." Her article accused board members not only of neglecting the schools, but also of giving young black women jobs in return for sexual favors.

To criticize the very board members who hired her was risky. In hopes of lessening the chance of being fired, she inserted the name of her co-owner, Taylor Nightingale, as the author of the article, then showed him the proofs for his approval. He refused to take credit. The essay may have seemed too bold even to him; or perhaps he was merely irked that Wells had inserted his name before asking permission. But the piece was already set in type; the deadline loomed. The best Wells could do was remove Nightingale's name and let the essay run anonymously.

It created a "sensation," she recalled, provoking "much comment." One newspaper "openly stated that the charges were true that some of our teachers took walks and rides with friends of the other race." Although Wells had raised just that possibility, to have the charge flung back and casually asserted as truth made her angry. *Some* of our teachers? Unsubstantiated rumors like that had dogged her ever since the whispers in Holly Springs about her taking money from white men. Angrily she threw back the gauntlet, demanding in the *Free Speech* that any accuser with reliable evidence supply the specific names of the teachers. To make vague accusations of such breathtaking sweep "put all forty of our public school teachers under suspicion."[46]

"Agitate and act until something is done," Wells insisted. Yet who could predict how every act would play out? Not long after issuing her demand for names, Ida looked out one evening onto the bright, moonlit street outside her apartment. A young black woman was strolling along. By her side—close by her side— walked a young man who was white. Ida knew the fellow. He was a lawyer for the board of education. As for the woman, she was in her early twenties and beautiful. A veil covered her face. But a veil could not conceal the woman's characteristic walk, nor her clothing. It was the same dress she had worn earlier in the day at Clay Street School, where Ida taught. The woman's classroom, in fact, stood directly next to Ida's.

Miss Hattie Britton. The sight took Ida's breath away. Miss Hattie was one of the younger teachers, twenty-three years old. More to the point, Ida was friends with three of her sisters. The oldest, nearly forty, was none other than Julia Britton Hooks—the accomplished pianist at whose soirée Ida had recited a speech by Lady Macbeth— and the woman who had won Ida's admiration for protesting seg-regated seating in Memphis theaters. Hattie was now boarding with Mrs. Hooks on Lauderdale Street, not far from Ida's resi-dence. Mrs. Hooks was one of the most respected black teachers in the city. She also had been principal of the Clay Street School.

Ida had met another of Hattie's sisters, Meb, at the press con-vention in Louisville. Like Ida, Meb was a journalist, writing the women's column for the *Lexington Herald*. The two women took an immediate fancy to each other—so much so that they spent much of the convention together. Meb called at Ida's lodgings along with another sister, the well-to-do Mrs. Susan Britton Franklin, who invited them both to spend a day at her nearby country seat.[47] There Ida was served "the finest dinner…the most superb I ever ate" before coming back to Louisville and staying the night with Meb. Perhaps it had been that evening when this younger sister delivered what Ida judged to be "the best recitation of ''Ostler Joe' I've heard."

> I stood at eve, as the sun went down, by a grave where a woman lies,
> Who lured men's souls to the shores of sin with the light of
> her wanton eyes…[48]

Now Hattie Britton had become entangled with this white lawyer. She had become, in fact, one of the women whose name Ida had demanded be published to the world in disgrace, in order to preserve the honor of those black teachers so indiscriminately accused. *They say.*

The two saw each other every day in school. Surely Hattie had read Ida's articles. Did she speak of them? Did Ida tell Hattie that she knew of her liaison or entreat her to break it off? Did Hattie feel guilty about the relationship, whether or not Ida confronted her? Was she being coerced? Or was she genuinely in love with the man and he with her? Was he already married to a respectable white woman? Or would he have been willing, let us say, to cut Miss Britton's fingers and suck, so he could swear that black blood flowed through his veins? Idle questions, the answers to which are beyond knowing. Wells set down the only account of her involvement nearly forty years later. The memories were still vivid, though she never mentioned Hattie Britton by name. "But this beautiful young girl carried on her clandestine love affair with this young white man, growing bolder as time went on. One Sunday morning she came to her sister's home after having been out all night and was charged by her brother-in-law with immoral practice." That would have been Mrs. Hooks's husband, Thomas. According to a brief notice on the front page of the *Detroit Plaindealer*, ACCUSED OF IMMORALITY, Mr. and Mrs. Hooks and Miss Hattie Britton were just leaving their house for church when Thomas confronted her. As Ida recalled, "In the bitter scene which ensued he called her some hard names. She ran to her room, snatched a pistol out of her trunk, rammed it as far into her ear as it would go and blew her brains out. It was significant to look at the floral pieces that were sent to her funeral—the largest and finest had the name of her admirer boldly attached to it."[49]

❦

So the article on black schools, with its unsparing tones and sharp angles, bit back in unexpected ways. The essay took a second bite at summer's end, when the new school year began. Only then did Wells learn that the board had not renewed her contract. It had said nothing all summer, so she would have no time to find another position.

Wells now faced her own crisis. Her salary as editor of the *Free Speech* was small compared with her income from teaching. Circulation hovered around fifteen hundred copies a week, producing not enough income to support her. Worse, Taylor Nightingale had become embroiled in a controversy with his congregation at Beale Street Baptist Church, which ended with him departing for Oklahoma. Wells and her remaining partner, J. L. Fleming, were forced to buy out his share of the *Free Speech*.[50] With Nightingale gone, fewer members of his church were buying the paper every Sunday.

Faced with declining circulation, Wells looked for solutions. She had the help of Isaiah Montgomery, a new acquaintance from Mississippi. Since 1887, Montgomery had directed efforts to create a black agricultural community at Mound Bayou, in the Delta region. Why not sell subscriptions in Mound Bayou and elsewhere in the Delta? he asked. Give the paper a broader circulation base. Ida plunged into the project with characteristic zeal. Ironically, she succeeded in part thanks to subsidies from the very railroads that had long discriminated against her. In that ruthlessly competitive era, rail lines craved favorable publicity and regularly supplied journalists with free passes. Wells discovered the practice in 1887 when William Simmons used them to pay her way to Louisville. A journalist simply applied to the local railroad superintendent, who had the power to grant travel for an appropriate period free of charge.

Contacting friends like Isaiah Montgomery in Mound Bayou, Wells arranged invitations to the meetings of any notable group in town, whether church councils, political gatherings, or Masonic conventions. She would step to the head of the assembly and tell the audience that as black folk, they needed to be informed, keep in touch, stand together. Listeners who had heard of "Iola" or Miss Ida B. Wells were delighted to meet her in person. Those who hadn't met her, found it arresting to hear a female editor stump for subscriptions as well as file stories about the goings-on in

A railroad pass

their towns. To cement the ties, Wells appointed a correspondent to send in weekly reports, so the news would continue to come. When she had collected her subscriptions, she asked her hosts to introduce her to someone in the next town down the line.

Success was infectious. Walk into the Masonic Lodge of Water Valley, Mississippi, and the grand master halted the meeting to give her half an hour. She came out with so many silver dollars, she was forced to proceed immediately to a bank. At the state bar association of black attorneys in Greenville, her talk yielded subscriptions from "every man present." As Ida traveled the railroads, she saw that many newspapers used "news butchers" to distribute their issues to towns and villages. One of the men couldn't help noticing the *Free Speech*'s popularity. He'd "never known so many colored people to ask for a newspaper before" and asked if he could distribute her paper. She agreed.

Since more than a few buyers of the *Free Speech* were not literate and got others to read the paper to them, Wells hit on the idea of printing issues on pink paper, to make them easily identifiable. Especially along the spur line to the Delta, news butchers found themselves besieged by requests for "the pink paper." Less honest agents who didn't carry the *Free Speech* fobbed off copies of the *Police Gazette*, which was the same color.[51]

Perhaps because Wells was able to get out and speak more with ordinary folk, the talk at various conventions began to seem ineffective, even a bit windy. She supported the Afro-American League, but after attending its gathering in Knoxville, she was in no mood for mere speeches. What had been accomplished, she wanted to know?

> It seems to me that some explicit work should have been mapped out for the ensuing year...If the league had gone out from its meeting with a pledge to fight the separate car law...enlist the ministers' help, to pledge every Negro to stay off railroads except when absolutely necessary—the next annual meeting would find an increased membership, renewed enthusiasm, and the moral support of numbers so necessary to create public sentiment.
>
> A handful of men, with no report of work accomplished, no one in the field to spread it, no plan of work laid out—no intelligent direction—meet and by their child's play illustrate in their own doings the truth of the saying that Negroes have no capacity for organization. Meanwhile a whole race is lynched, proscribed, intimidated, deprived of its political and civil rights, herded into boxes (by courtesy called separate cars) which bring the blush of humiliation to every self-respecting man's cheek—and we sit tamely by without using the only means—that of thorough organization and earnest work to prevent it. No wonder the world at large spits upon us with impunity.[52]

Only a month later word came from Georgetown, Kentucky, of a different response to a lynching. Someone in the black community struck back, setting fires at two judges' residences and a nearby college. White Southerners were horrified; whites in Memphis even more so when they discovered the *Free Speech* praising the fires as a "true spark of manhood." Wells's voice came through like a clap of thunder. "We had begun to think the Negroes…hadn't manhood enough in them to wriggle and crawl out of the way, much less protect and defend themselves…Not until the Negro rises in his might and takes a hand resenting such cold-blooded murders, if he has to burn up whole towns, will a halt be called in wholesale lynching."[53]

Wells kept searching for ways to act—more effective than speech making, less drastic than arson. She called for a boycott of one Memphis paper whose race baiting had become particularly harsh. She continued to create a network of correspondents with her paper as the nerve center. By March 1892, circulation had jumped from fifteen hundred to four thousand, a rise of over 250 percent. Wells's salary increased to within ten dollars of what she had once earned from teaching. "I was handed from town to town from Memphis to Natchez, Mississippi, and treated like a queen," she recalled.

Ida was in Natchez, over three hundred miles from home, still expanding the reach of her paper, when news from Memphis came humming along the telegraph wires and bursting from the headlines, tossed off at each depot by the news butchers:

A BLOODY RIOT

Deputies Shot By Negroes
A Horrible Affair at the Curve Late Last Night

The headlines trumpeted an unambiguous message in type set in black and white. But for Ida, its significance swirled and blurred at a distance of several hundred miles. The words on the page were black, but the papers were owned by whites. A "Bloody Riot"—what did that mean? "Deputies Shot By Negroes."

They Say. Whatever the meaning, one message was clear. Drop everything. Come home—now.

· Six ·

THEY SAY

❦—❦

SATURDAY, MARCH 5

A BLOODY RIOT

Deputies Shot By Negroes
A Horrible Affair at the Curve Late Last Night
The Condition of Deputy Sheriff Cole Very Serious—The
Others Will Recover—A Large Lot of Weapons Captured.
The Dive Long Known as a Disturbance Breeder—A Full
Account of the Affair

T HREE DEPUTY SHERIFFS SHOT. ONE OF THEM WILL DIE, AND
another is very badly hurt.

Thirteen negroes are immured in cells at the station house.

It all resulted from the existence of a nest of turbulent and
unruly negroes living in the neighborhood of the "Curve," just
outside the city line, where Mississippi Avenue merges into the
Hernando road and the street-cars turn to go to Elmwood.

For years the Curve has been notorious for the character of
the negroes who reside nearby, and of late they have become
more turbulent than ever. On Wednesday the second of March
a negro youth named Armour Harris assaulted the child of

Cornelius Hurst, an express messenger. Hurst caught Armour and thrashed him.

Afterwards a crowd of negroes gathered in front of a grocery near where Hurst lives, and discussed the propriety of lynching the white man. They were practically a unit in favor of doing so, but Hurst was known to be good grit and the dusky avengers couldn't decide who should lead an attack on his house. W. H. Barrett, the owner of the grocery, tried to quiet them, and was set upon and clubbed and shot at, several bullets passing through his clothes. The assault occurred in "The People's Grocery," an establishment owned by a stock company of negroes and run by Calvin McDowell.

McDowell was arrested Thursday and gave bond for his appearance at the Criminal Court. Since then the negroes have been holding secret meetings and evidently preparing for trouble. At 8 o'clock Friday they met in a church, near the Curve, and listened to incendiary speeches. Yesterday they boasted to white residents that no deputy sheriff dare attempt to arrest them.

Judge DuBose was appealed to, and he issued a bench warrant for Armour Harris and Will Stuart, and instructed Deputy Sheriffs Perkins, Cole, and Harold to arrest the negroes, also to suppress any riotous assembly around the Curve. The officers called on nine other men and proceeded at 10 o'clock Saturday night.

Everything seemed as quiet as a May morning, but when the posse entered Barrett's store he told the members to be careful when they entered the People's Grocery, as they might be ambushed. The officers thought Barrett was unnecessarily alarmed, but took the precaution to divide, and one party went to the back door of the negro grocery.

Joe Perkins, Bob Harold, Charley Cole, and Avery Yerger went to the front door. Calvin McDonald was pacing up and down the floor. Several other negroes, among them Ned Trigg, a mail carrier, and Hugh Williams, were standing behind the counter.

Perkins was in front and asked McDowell if Will Stuart were there.

"He's in the back room," replied McDowell.

As Perkins walked into the back room, leaving Cole, Harold, and Yerger standing in the door, the other deputies entered by a back door.

Bang! Bang! Bang!

A volley of shots was heard by the officers in the back room. They supposed that the fighting had begun in front and charged on a group of negroes who were partly concealed by a screen. The negroes were armed with shotguns, but the officers closed in on them and used their pistols as clubs. In the space of a minute the negroes in the back room had dropped their guns and those who could fled.

Then the officers in the rear discovered what had befallen Cole, Yerger, and Harold. No sooner had the negroes who were behind the counter heard the posse enter from behind than they lifted shotguns concealed behind the counter and fired at the deputies in front. Each of the three officers was struck in the face or the head.

Charley Cole was desperately wounded. One of his eyes was out, but he strove gamely to draw his pistol and return the fire. The weapon caught in his pocket, and he ran into the street. Pete Bishop, who had stopped at Barrett's, heard the shooting and Cole's cries and rushed out just in time to see a negro advancing on Cole. Bishop had a shotgun and fired twice at the negro, who fell.

Bishop, seeing that Cole was badly wounded, assisted him to the residence of Cole's cousin on Shaw Avenue, then returned to the scene. The negro he shot had disappeared, but it is thought that he was badly hurt. The officers had three negroes including Calvin McDowell under arrest, but Trigg and Williams, who are believed to have begun the shooting, had escaped. The officers had also captured six shotguns, one Winchester rifle, and four revolvers that the negroes had in the back room.

The police station was telephoned to for help and the patrol wagon dispatched. A reporter from the *Appeal-Avalanche* rode along.

It was a wild scene that greeted the bluecoats as the wagon pulled up in front of Barrett's grocery. A crowd of 20 or 30 white men armed with shotguns, rifles, and revolvers surrounded four negro prisoners, who stood ankle deep in mud, with irons on their wrists and quaking with terror. There were ominous mutterings and suggestions about ropes and lamp posts, and it only needed an outright proposition to have secured a lynching bee right then. The police were as indignant as the others, but they did their duty and put the prisoners under guard.

A posse then visited the negro church, where some of the rioters were supposed to have barricaded themselves. There was no one in the church, but a search of a number of negro cabins resulted in the arrest of four more negroes, among them Armour Harris, the young viper who brought on the whole trouble. His father was one of the crowd in the grocery during the shooting, but he could not be found. The mother of the boy was full of ginger, and abused the officers roundly for invading her house.

As the posse marched off with Armour handcuffed to a big yellow negro, who was caught on the highway with a revolver in his pocket, the virago shrieked out: "'March on like a soldier, Armour, de lawd's wid you an' agin de white folks."

Several other homes were visited and additional suspects taken, then the *Appeal-Avalanche* man returned to town. At 3 o'clock everything was quiet at the Curve.

MONDAY, MARCH 7

The affair of Saturday night at the Curve is without a parallel in the criminal annals of this section of the country.

Men have been ambushed and murdered, white men have been slain by negro mobs, and officers have been shot down while in the discharge of their duty, but there is no other instance on record of a posse of officers acting under the orders of a court of record, and proceeding quietly and peaceably to execute warrants charging individuals with the commission of small offenses being led into an ambush and subjected to the murderous fire of a band of negroes who were without a grievance, and were actuated solely by race prejudices and a vicious and venomous rancor against the representatives of the law that seeks to hold their brutal passions in check.

Yesterday the Curve was not a good location for the colored man unless he was peacefully and respectfully disposed. White men stood around in groups and discussed the outrage of the night before and plans to bring the turbulent negroes in the neighborhood to a proper sense of the proprieties. Some members of every group carried Winchesters or shotguns, and their bloodshot eyes and haggard faces showed that they had been up all night.

About 4 o'clock yesterday morning Patrolman Perry and Deputy Sheriff Richardson captured Tom Moss the president of the corporation that owns the People's Grocery.

Moss is the man who shot Charlie Cole, not Trigg, as was stated yesterday. Both men are letter carriers, and have been rather numerous in the disturbances that have occurred from time to time at the Curve, and those circumstances led to a confusion of names. There is no doubt as to Moss' guilt. Mr. Cole stated yesterday that he saw Moss shoot him. Cole was standing in the front door of the store and Moss was behind the counter. There was a gun fired in the back room and almost at the same instant Cole saw Moss level a gun at him and fire. He was blinded, and turned and ran out of the door, endeavoring as he did to draw his pistol.

Moss, when arrested, said to Patrolman Perry, "How many were killed?"

"Three white men," replied Perry.

"All them God damned sons of bitches of deputy sheriffs ought to have been killed," said Moss.

Moss is a brown-skinned negro, 24 years old, and wears a beard. He talks well, and bears a noticeable resemblance to Andrew Jackson, who killed one white man and wounded another in the lower part of this county something over two years ago, and who was to have been hanged last August, but whose sentence was commuted by Governor Buchanan.

Moss asserted that he didn't know anything about the affair. He denied shooting Cole, and denied that he said the deputies ought to have been killed. It is pretty well established that he did say it, however, and there is no doubt that he shot Cole.

Nat Trigg, the other mail carrier, whose identity got confounded with Moss, was also arrested early in the morning. He denied all knowledge of the affair, but he is in jail just the same. Ten other negroes were arrested during the day and taken to jail. There are 26 under arrest, and only two who are still at large and badly wanted. They are Shank Shields and Hugh Williams.

Shields shot Deputy Bob Harold and Avery Yerger and is believed to have fired the first shot. He is a desperate fellow and is expected to show fight when found by the men who are searching for him. They will capture him alive, if convenient.

Attorney-General Peters, in speaking of the affair yesterday, commended the conduct of the officers highly, giving them great credit for the self-control they exhibited in not killing the negroes instead of capturing them. The attorney general had a gleam in his eye, however, that indicated a determination to make the captives wish they had been put to death before they encountered the Criminal Court.

The proofs that the negroes had deliberately planned a wholesale slaughter of white men were apparent to all who visited the People's Grocery Store yesterday. That they did not carry out their purpose to murder every man in the sheriff's posse is due to a lack of courage rather than the absence of will or ability. The walls in the back room of the store are riddled with shot and the stovepipe has a hole in it big enough to shove an egg in, where a load of shot and slugs struck it.

Judge DuBose read about the riot in the *Appeal-Avalanche* yesterday morning and then went out to the Curve and took a look at the scene. He encouraged the officers to proceed with the work of capturing the miscreants.

There was a strong guard of white men at the Curve last night, and about 9 o'clock it was reported that negroes were organizing at a church, some two miles out on the Hernando road. It was a false alarm, but if the negroes had come they would have been warmly received. There is little or no likelihood of further trouble. The negroes in the Curve neighborhood know that another outbreak would result disastrously for them, and they will remain quiet.

TUESDAY, MARCH 8

The affairs of the Curve wore a very placid aspect on the surface yesterday. But there was an undercurrent of uneasiness and apprehension pervading both white and black citizens in that vicinity. The white people discussed the situation with grave faces, and they went about prepared for any emergency that might be the outcome of the doings of Saturday night. The colored people lay very low. There were officers in the neighborhood all day, ferreting out participants in the shooting, and all the negroes whose consciences were not easy made themselves very scarce. The only arrest made was of George Thornton. While it is not known that Thornton was one of the ambushers, it is generally understood that he was at the head of the incendiary meeting that was held by the negroes on the night before the affray. He called the meeting and made the first speech when it assembled.

At 10 o'clock last night deputies brought into custody Isaiah Johnson, alias "Shang," who had been found eight miles east of Memphis. Johnson is the negro who fired both barrels of the shotgun at Deputies Bob Harrell and Avery Yerger with such good effect. He declined to make any statement and would not talk after arriving at the jail. The arrest completes the good work of the officers, who now have in custody all of the principals of Saturday night's riot, except Hugh Williams, and he cannot remain at large much longer.

WEDNESDAY, MARCH 9

Calvin McDowell, Tom Moss and Will Stewart, ringleaders in the assault on the deputies who raided the Curve last Saturday night, are missing from their cells in Shelby County jail this morning.

At 2:30 o'clock this morning they were removed by a band of 75 men wearing masks.

What has become of the three negroes is known only to the men who took them from the jail, but it is a reasonable inference that long ere this, Judge Lynch has passed sentence upon them, and that the sentence has been executed.

About 3 o'clock this morning a telephone call on the *Appeal-Avalanche* announced that the jail had been entered, and some of the "Curve" rioters removed by masked men. When the representative of the *Appeal-Avalanche* arrived at the jail he found a solemn looking group at the gate. Watchman O'Donnell said, "At 2 o'clock this morning I was sitting in the office of the jail with Mr. Seat talking. I heard a ring at the gate, and went to the door of the jail asking who was there.

"'Hugh Williams, of Whitehaven,' came the reply. 'I have a prisoner.'"

"'All right,' I replied, 'and this is the place and I am always ready to receive them.'" With that Mr. O'Donnell hurried to the gate and unlocked it. Two or three men pushed in immediately. The men were masked.

"What does this mean?" queried the brave watchman as he reached for his pistol.

"No, you don't," exclaimed the masked men loudly as they seized the arms of Mr. O'Donnell.

The three men who seized Mr. O'Donnell evidently had spoken loudly as they grasped him, for their voices had scarcely died away when there was a trampling of many feet, and fully 75 men, all wearing black masks, rushed through the gate and confronted the astounded watchman.

"We want the keys to the cells in which these negroes are confined," came sternly from the leader of the masked avengers. They entered the jail and when they found the keys, made a circuit of the jail, searching for the men they wanted. Ghostly their steps sounded as they trod the corridors, peering into cell after cell. Some of the prisoners who had been aroused from slumber stared in horror as fierce eyes from beneath the black masks glared in upon them.

The intruders passed by cell after cell till they came to Calvin McDowell's. He was wanted.

Then came Will Stewart and Tom Moss.

What passed between the avengers and the doomed as the latter were roused from sleep and ordered to come, only those parties know, for Watchman O'Donnell was in the outer yard, pinioned and under guard.

But whatever entreaties, what tears, may have come from the doomed rioters, they were unavailing, for the prisoners passed from their cells into the keeping of the somber-masked avengers. Not a word did they say as they passed the bound watchman, but like phantoms of the night, they trooped through the gate. Which way they turned O'Donnell doesn't know. All he does know is that as soon as the echoes of their footsteps had died away, the two men who had been guarding him bucked off and also disappeared.

All efforts, at that hour, of the newspaper men to trace the mob were vain. Just as this is being written a telephone message says that the negroes were hanged in the Chesapeake & Ohio rail yards, and that there were five of them instead of three.

The affair was one of the most orderly of its kind ever conducted, judging from the accounts. There was no whooping, not even loud talking, no cursing, in fact nothing boisterous. Everything was done decently and in order.

The vengeance was sharp, swift, and sure, but administered with due regard to the fact that people were asleep all around the jail, and that it is not good form to arouse people from their slumbers at 3 o'clock in the morning.

Not a gun was fired, not a shout was heard. Until they read it in this morning's *Appeal-Avalanche*, the people living in the vicinity of the jail will not know that the avengers swooped down last night and sent the murderous souls of the ringleaders in the Curve riot into eternity.

Thursday, March 10

There is no clew to the identity of any member of the mob that lynched McDowell, Moss and Stuart. There were probably 75 men in the party, and the impression obtains pretty generally that nearly all of them were from the country.

Never were the plans of a mob more carefully and skillfully executed. The flight was so rapid and orderly that not a ripple of excitement or comment was created along the line of march, although the body of lynchers was observed by several persons along the way. Sheriff McLendon made an investigation along the route, and he was led to believe that the mob fell off along the road or divided into two or more parts. The watchman at the gasworks north of the jail saw the crowd and estimated the number at about 75, the same figure stated by Watchman O'Donnell at the jail. At other places along the railroad the gang was seen, the observers nearest the starting place estimating the number at much higher figures than those nearer the scene of the killing, the latter fixing the number at from 20 to 30.

Inspector Walker, whose business calls him to the vicinity of the scene of the tragedy, heard firing in the nearby field but paid no attention to it, and when he saw a number of men coming down the track a few minutes later, he supposed they were tramps who had stole their way into the city on the freight train. He could see nothing but their shadows as they passed, but counted eight of them as they passed along. He thinks that these were the extent of the gang of lynchers, but he may be mistaken about that, inasmuch as persons living in the neighborhood also heard a gang of men rush to the Randolph road immediately after and drive toward the city in wagons.

The men who went back to the city along the railroad track retained their masks at least part of the way. They were seen by a crew of railroad men in the yards, who say that they wore white masks, though of what material they could not tell. Watchman O'Donnell says that the masks consisted merely of handkerchiefs fastened over their faces.

It was about 4 o'clock yesterday morning when a party of five men, including police officers, picked their way gingerly along the Chesapeake & Ohio Railroad with the aid of a dim lantern. They found a bonfire burning just opposite the old waterworks plants alongside the railroad tracks, and around this fire were three negroes. The officers surrounded the trio and searched them in the expectation of finding concealed weapons. But the weapons were not there.

"Where was that shooting in the neighborhood a little while ago?" demanded Jimmy Cox, one of the men.

"Boss, we don't know nothing about the shooting," replied one negro. "We were lying here when it was done. It sounded off in that direction," pointing over the hill.

Those negroes had lain snugly up to the fire while the triple tragedy was being enacted, and did not consider the sound of a hundred shots, fired not more than 200 yards away, a matter of sufficient importance to demand an investigation. The posse went rapidly in the direction pointed by the negroes and had gone just over an intervening knoll when they came upon the scene.

It was at the bottom of a ravine that slopes toward Wolf River, in an open field of about ten acres. On the east is the Randolph road; on the west the Chesapeake & Ohio tracks, which at that point lie atop an embankment some eight or ten feet high.

The bodies lay in the center of this field close to the bed of a dried up stream. The soil is clayey, and there are clumps of verdure here and there. The posse that found the bodies might have walked right past the spot in darkness if they had not carried the lantern by whose pale and flickering rays they were able to locate the corpses.

They were the bodies of Calvin McDowell, Will Stewart, and Tom Moss.[1]

Seven

Do Something

✦━✦

N<small>O DOUBT SHE WOULD HAVE COME HOME IN ANY CASE, GIVEN</small> the latest run of headlines.

LYNCHED!

Memphis Jail Broken Open
Three of the Curve Rioters
Taken Out by Masked Men

What made her drop everything, though, was Tommie.

Thomas Moss was as good a friend as any Ida had in Memphis. She had gotten to know him partly because he was a letter carrier—a job coveted in the African American community, a federal position, and one that paid decently. Moss delivered the mail to the *Free Speech* offices, so he saw Ida almost daily. Above and beyond the letters, he reported the talk of the town, incidents in the neighborhood, any clashes with police. Ida knew him from Avery Chapel as well, where both taught Sunday school. Tommie was quiet, polite, well spoken. He and his wife Betty had asked Ida to be godmother to their young daughter Maurine.[1]

LYNCHED!

Memphis Jail Broken Open

Three of the Curve Rioters Taken Out by Masked Men.

McDowell, Moss and Stewart the Victims of the Mob.

Seventy-five Men Assault the Jail at 2:30 O'Clock This Morning.

The Watchman Is Seized and Tied with Ropes.

The Entrance to the Cells Then Effected Without Trouble.

There Was No Noise or Other Disturbance —The Direction Taken by the Mob Not Ascertained, But the Negroes Are Probably Hanging Somewhere This Morning.

Calvin McDowell, —— Moss and Will Stewart, ringleaders in the assault on the deputies who raided the Curve last Saturday night, are missing from their cells in Shelby County Jail this morning.

At 2:30 o'clock this morning they were removed by a band of 75 men wearing masks.

What has become of the three negroes is known only to the men who took them from the jail, but it is a reasonable inference that long ere this Judge Lynch has passed sentence upon them, and that the sentence has been executed.

of you, d—n you," retorted the gritty watchman.

All this while the keys for which they were asking were lying on the table in the jailor's office.

Strangely enough the avengers in their first search had entered the office, but had overlooked the keys, which were partly concealed by a paper that had been carelessly thrown upon the table.

For the second time the avengers entered the jail. Not many minutes after their entrance a subdued shout of "here they are," informed O'Donnell that the keys had been found.

Then the avengers made a circuit of the jail, searching for the men they wanted. Ghostly their steps sounded as they trod the corridors, peering into cell after cell. Some of the prisoners who had been aroused from slumber stared in horror as the black masked faces from which shone fierce eyes glared in upon them.

They passed by cell after cell till they came to Calvin McDowell's. He was wanted.

Then came Will Stewart and Tom Moss. What passed between the avengers and the doomed as the latter were roused from sleep and ordered to come, only those parties know, for Watchman O'Donnell was in the outer yard, fast pinioned and under guard, and Jailer Williams was still sleeping the sleep of the just.

But whatever may have passed, what entreaties, what tears, may have come from the doomed rioters, they were unavailing, for they passed from their cells into the keeping of the sombre-masked avengers.

Then as Watchman O'Donnell tells it, the masked men and their prey came trooping out.

Not a word did they say as they passed the bound watchman, but like phantoms of the night, they trooped through the gate. Which way they turned after leaving the jail, to the right or to the left, O'Donnell doesn't know. All he does know is that as soon as the echoes of their footsteps had died away, the two men who had been guarding him backed off and also disappeared.

The lead story in the Memphis Appeal-Avalanche, *March 9, 1892*

Now he was dead—a "turbulent, unruly negro," one of a "nest of vipers" who had planned a wholesale slaughter of white men and whose execution by a mob had been sharp, swift, and sure.

The train journey from Natchez seemed interminable. What had happened? Who could tell? The papers were full of accounts, the column inches of text spilling across the page, thrown together at breakneck speed into a tale of lurid clarity never wavering in its conviction that the town's Negroes were brutal criminals, shrieking viragos, ready to riot upon the slightest pretext. Yet the bold strokes, the confident assertions shimmered like a mirage, as one incontrovertible detail or another disappeared in the blink of an eye, to be replaced by some new assertion, equally incontrovertible, yet in opposition to what had been said before. Ned Trigg and Hugh Williams began the shooting. No, it was Tom Moss who was the ringleader and pulled the trigger, not Trigg. That was beyond a doubt. Charley Cole said so.

Cole had his eye shot out and was so seriously wounded, he would die. Actually Cole could see well enough to identify Moss as his assailant. He would recover.

Shank Shields shot Deputy Bob Harold and Deputy Avery Yerger. Actually it was Shang, not Shank, and Johnson, not Shields. Isaiah Johnson shot Harold and Yerger. It was Johnson, alias Shang.

Three men were hanged by the lynchers. Five men were hanged. No, three men were shot.

A mob of seventy-five people trooped into the jail wearing black masks and, like phantoms, extracted their prisoners without any loud talking, cursing, or whooping. Their flight was so rapid and orderly, not a ripple of excitement was created.

Actually, there were more than a hundred gunshots fired. Inspector Walker, whose business it was to enforce the law, heard firing in the nearby field and paid no attention to it. But three unarmed Negroes (searched upon suspicion of carrying concealed weapons) were held up to scorn for not having gone to investigate.

Actually, the lynchers may have numbered only twenty to thirty. They were wearing white masks, not black. No, they were only wearing handkerchiefs tied around their faces. And the party may have been only about eight people.

Ida could know little for certain until she reached Memphis. One red flag waved most disturbingly, however: the name of W. H. Barrett, the white man who "tried to quiet" the blacks protesting Cornelius Hurst's beating of Armour Harris—the same Barrett who warned the sheriff's deputies that there might be an ambush waiting in the People's Grocery. Barrett had long born a grudge against Tommie, for an obvious reason. He owned the store across the way that directly competed with the People's Grocery.

Small groceries were a fixture of cities and towns across the South. They sold provisions of all sorts—flour, eggs, butter, meats—but they also served as places to gather and socialize. People needing lunch might buy cheese and crackers for a nickel or crackers and oysters for a dime.[2] On Saturday nights when working folk had time off, men came in to talk, play cards, gamble, and drink, for most such establishments sold liquor as well. Robert Church, the black Memphis entrepreneur and philanthropist, launched his path to respectability and wealth by running a grocery store. Indeed, he had been left for dead on the floor while defending it during the race riots of 1866. Tommie Moss used savings from his day job to open his store at the Curve. His manager, Calvin McDowell, and his clerk, Will Stewart, kept shop during the day. Evenings Tommie came to help and tot up the books. About ten African Americans in all were stockholders in the business.[3]

They called it the People's Grocery and perhaps there was an edge to the name. Until the grocery opened in 1889, the neighborhood had no alternative but to depend on W. H. Barrett's store, which stood across the way on the southwest corner of the Curve, where streetcars turned off Hernando Road. Moss was convinced he could garner a profitable business. He was a respected member of his church and his fraternal lodge and he charged less for his goods. Even some whites patronized the store.[4]

Barrett did not take kindly to competition from a couple of young black "boys." Moss was only twenty-four and McDowell and Stewart were in their early twenties—healthy, well built, confident. McDowell, six feet tall, was a member of the Tennessee Rifles, a black militia that had been formed about five years earlier.

CALVIN McDOWELL.
MURDERED BY THE MEMPHIS MOB.

McDowell, as he appeared in an African American newspaper, the St. Paul Appeal, *March 26, 1892*

The Rifles drilled regularly and were supported by contributions from the local community.[5]

To Ida, Barrett seemed a likely agitator in any disturbance around the Curve. Indeed, when she finally spoke to Betty Moss and others close to the situation, she found that the white storekeeper had been in the thick of the controversy. On Wednesday, March 2, a mixed group of boys had been playing marbles when a quarrel broke out, primarily between Armour Harris and the son of Cornelius Hurst. Armour got the better of the fight and sent young Hurst packing. Then the white father came looking for Armour and thrashed him, enraged that a colored boy had whipped his son. In response, Harris's father and several companions demanded an explanation. Harsh words were traded and a crowd gathered. Barrett, whose store was just down the street, joined Hurst's defenders. Calvin McDowell and Will Stewart supported the Harrises.

Barrett next fetched a police officer, who brought a warrant for the arrest of one of the principals, probably Harris. The two whites entered the People's Grocery, Barrett demanding that McDowell turn over the suspect. When McDowell denied knowing his whereabouts, Barrett pulled out his revolver and clubbed him to the floor, hitting so hard, the gun spun from his hand and skittered across the planking. While Will Stewart held off the deputy, Calvin lunged for the weapon and fired at Barrett, by this time in full retreat. The officer arrested McDowell who, after a night in jail, posted bond.[6]

The Curve was up in arms. Black residents met Friday night, irate over the harassment inflicted whenever their behavior was deemed "impudent" or "sassy," sick of the lynchings constantly reported in the papers. In the latest quarrel, McDowell had been hauled off to jail while Barrett went scot-free after clubbing McDowell to the ground. Cornelius Hurst had been ignored when he beat up young Armour Harris. Furthermore, the day before the fight at the Curve, the proprietor of a small restaurant downtown, Zeb Nolan, had gotten thoroughly liquored and stood outside the Louisville and Nashville depot, insulting "every negro that passed." He knocked the hat off one man and then hit a black letter carrier, Charley Mosby. Mosby knew Nolan all too well, tried to laugh it off and make his escape, but when a railroad porter laughed too, Nolan whirled and shot and wounded him twice, right in front of the Peabody Hotel. As police took Nolan away, he begged them to let him "kill the damned nigger." The *Appeal-Avalanche* treated the story as tongue-in-cheek entertainment: ZEB NOLAN ON THE WARPATH, read the headline.[7]

One or two speakers at the meeting got hot: they called for "cleaning out the 'damned white trash' with dynamite."[8] Meanwhile, whites in the neighborhood were angry and frightened. Any meeting the black community held was taken as a sign of conspiracy tantamount to riot. On Saturday, Barrett gathered up the rumors he'd heard and took them to Judge DuBose. White people feared for their safety, he said; already three families had moved out temporarily, for fear of reprisals. He asked that warrants be issued to pick up the troublemakers who had made incendiary threats. DuBose authorized a posse of deputies to make arrests.

Barrett went one step further, as Ida learned from her friends. He warned McDowell and Stewart that they had better watch out, a mob was coming to "clean out" the People's Grocery that evening.[9]

McDowell and Tommie Moss took the threat seriously. But what to do—summon the police? The idea was absurd, even without knowing that Barrett had arranged for warrants to be served. Moss consulted a lawyer, who noted that the store sat nearly a mile beyond the city line and therefore beyond the jurisdiction of the police. The People's Grocery, he suggested, would be entirely within its rights to defend itself from any mob.

This was no doubt what Barrett wanted: to provoke a fight, put his competitors in jail, and run their store out of business. The sheriff's posse arrived quietly, around ten thirty, none wearing uniforms. They went directly to Barrett, who warned them there might be an ambush. They divided their forces, sending half quietly around the back, while the rest entered in front. It was closing time. Tommie Moss was reading a paper when the four menacing strangers appeared. McDowell was expecting the worst, and when more men stormed in from the back, the defenders of the store opened fire.[10]

So Barrett had his way. His competitors—Moss, Stewart, and McDowell—were rounded up along with any other black men who seemed suspicious, carried a weapon, or were "unruly." The police jailed more than two dozen African Americans. But when the lynch mob came, they knew which victims to take: the owners of the People's Grocery. The black community had anticipated such a possibility, of course. The Tennessee Rifles, the militia to which McDowell belonged (he was wearing his military fatigues when arrested), placed a guard outside the jail both Sunday and Monday nights, to forestall any lynching parties.[11]

Tuesday the papers brought word that Charley Cole, the deputy most seriously wounded, was recovering. A lynching in retaliation for the death of a white man seemed less likely. On the other hand, Judge DuBose was taking no chances. He believed blacks had entirely too many guns at their command. He ordered that all black residents be disarmed, including the Tennessee Rifles.

Whites broke into the armory where the militia stored its arms and confiscated them. When officers of the Tennessee Rifles protested, General Carnes, in command of the state militia, agreed that the confiscation had been unlawful but did nothing to stop it. Memphis officials told the Rifles that they should practice their drills using sticks.[12] As for those in jail, DuBose strictly forbid any contact with friends, relatives, or lawyers. Betty Moss brought food for her husband but was turned away. "Anyone can see them after three days," DuBose was reported to have said."[13] He was right about that.

The jail was therefore unprotected early Wednesday morning when the "avengers" approached at two thirty, in black masks or white, with or without prearrangement, whether seventy-five or thirty or eight. (The actual number, almost everyone came to agree, was no more than ten.) The jailer insisted he was unable to identify any of the mob and neither did anyone called before the grand jury. (If the lynchers were alleged, conveniently, to have come mostly "from the country," who could identify such a mob of strangers?)

Yet somehow, only a day after the murders, the *Memphis Commercial* obtained a breathless account of the victims' final moments. Near the jail were railroad tracks where a switch engine had been backed up. The lynching party put its prisoners aboard and drove it north a little more than a mile to a field near the city brickworks. The route was the same one Ida had taken so many times when teaching in Woodstock; the same line, a dozen miles down, where the C&O conductor had ejected her from the ladies car.

Upon a signal from the executioners, the switch engine let off steam and blew its whistle, to drown out at least some of the gunshots. Calvin McDowell did not go gently; he grabbed one of the men's pistols, even with his hands bound. He may even have managed to kill an assailant. Reports noted that there were four pools of blood on the ground and only three victims. A policeman was said to have "died suddenly" the day after the lynching under obscure circumstances. Whether or not McDowell managed the deed, he was punished for his "insolence" by having the fingers on his offending hand shot and mutilated as well as his eyes gouged out, leaving him so disfigured that the mourners who passed his casket gasped in horror. Tommie, the paper said, had begged for his life, for the sake of his wife and the unborn child she was carrying. His plea was scorned. He was asked only for his final words.

"Tell my people to go West—" he said, "there is no justice for them here."

The deputies found the bodies shortly before dawn—it could not have been many hours later. When they rolled Moss over, they discovered he was carrying papers in his back pocket. They were his Sunday school literature.[14]

Ida was unable to reach Memphis until after the funeral, held Thursday, April 10. The day before, when word spread that the bodies were being taken to Walsh, the undertaker, some two hundred African Americans surged into the streets to see for themselves. A frightened deputy reported the crowd to Judge DuBose,

Scene of the Lynching Looking East Toward Cubbin's Brick Yard.

A sketch from the Memphis Appeal-Avalanche, *March 10, 1892*

characterizing it as "hostile" and guessing that it was marching toward the Curve. DuBose ordered a hundred white men raised and armed. The reaction was almost festive. The *Appeal-Avalanche* had been posting handwritten bulletins outside its office and whites, reading them, raced to Kupperschmidt's Gun Store demanding to be outfitted according to the sheriff's orders. The store was quickly emptied of its firearms.

As the Linden and Magnolia trolleys traversed their usual route, the newly armed men jumped aboard and even clambered onto the trolley roofs, brandishing rifles, pistols, knives. This posse was joined by white residents at the Curve, but no black mob could be found. Even if blacks had wanted to strike back, as some did, they had few arms and the white "deputies" were allowed free rein. As they patrolled the streets, other rabble looted the People's Grocery, broke out its inventories of cigars and liquor, and destroyed about $1,800 worth of supplies. What was left was later sold by creditors at a fraction of its cost—to none other than W. H. Barrett.[15]

Emotions ran high during the funeral at Avery Chapel, where Tommie Moss and Ida had taught Sunday school. The ministers' prayers were regularly interrupted by shouts and sobs; the march to Mount Zion cemetery was perhaps the largest black procession in the city's history. Many residents left work to attend. At graveside, Betty Moss fainted—overcome by grief and by the finality of the occasion.

"Where is Hell?" asked the *Detroit Plaindealer,* and answered with a litany of lynching sites. "A few weeks ago it was in Virginia, then it drifted to Pine Bluff, Ark., then to Mississippi, Florida, Georgia, Louisiana, Texas, back to Arkansas, assuming a most horrible form at Texarkana, week before last. Last week it was at Memphis, Tenn." Wells objected. They were "doing the real hell an injustice. Hell proper is a place of punishment for the wicked—Memphis is a place of punishment for the good, brave and enterprising."[16]

She was too late to mourn at Tommie's funeral, too late even to walk in the procession to the grave. She sensed the mood of the town, however, both black and white. Despite white attempts to disarm the black community, she managed to buy a pistol. "I felt that one had better die fighting against injustice than to die like a dog or a rat in a trap."[17]

Ida Wells (left) a few years after the Memphis shootings, with Betty Moss and her two children, Maurine and Thomas, Jr., the latter named after his father

Despite the brave talk, the killings produced an almost claustrophobic sense of being trapped between grindstones with no room for maneuver. Protest at the ballot box? The state legislature had systematically rewritten it to suppress black voting. After the shootout at the Curve, the police had jailed Frank Schumann, the owner of Memphis' largest gun shop, for selling guns to blacks—only to throw open Kupperschmidt's shop later, to arm whites intent on subduing a nonexistent mob.[18] Do something. But what? Wells's initial reaction bordered on the biblical. In the *Free Speech* she wrote, "There is nothing we can do about the lynching now, as we are out-numbered and without arms…There is therefore only one thing left that we can do: save our money and leave a town which will neither protect our lives and property, nor give us a fair trial in the courts, but takes us out and murders us in cold blood when accused by white persons."[19] As Moses led his people out of Egypt, as Lot departed Sodom and Gomorrah, as black "Exodusters" fled the South at the end of Reconstruction—so African Americans should put Memphis behind them.

Black churches rallied their congregations. More than a thousand members attended a mass meeting to call for prosecution of the lynchers, to condemn the white press for inflaming public opinion, and to recommend emigration, to "seek among strangers the protection of just laws."[20] Some African Americans had long promoted a move to Liberia, as a return to their people's roots in Africa. But for most, Liberia seemed an impossibly ambitious destination. More appealing was Oklahoma Territory, which the federal government had formally opened to settlement in 1889. Whole congregations debated relocating and several did, including R. L. Countee's church. Another, Washington Baptist, upon departing sold its sanctuary to a local Jewish community.[21] Some folk could afford railroad tickets. Those who could not often traveled in groups, ferried across the Mississippi with open wagons in which the women and children rode, while the men walked the four-hundred-mile journey.

Some newspaper editors had invited Wells to relocate in the West, but her *Free Speech* partner, J. L. Fleming, was reluctant to go. Then, too, it was not easy to pick up everything and leave, especially for anyone with roots in the community. Another black newspaper, the *Memphis Reflector,* questioned the wisdom of mass emigration. "It is easy enough to cry go! go! but it takes a little longer to figure the cost."[22] After a few weeks, Wells began to see ways in which those remaining behind could make a difference, not so much through the legal system as in the economic sphere.

In mid-April, she received a visit from the superintendent and treasurer of the City Railway Company. The previous year the company had begun electrifying its trolley lines, not a small investment, and noticed recently that black ridership was falling off. Would Wells write an editorial, they inquired, reassuring her readers that the new electric trolleys were not dangerous and that conductors were specifically instructed to be civil to black riders?

Wells pointed out the connection the officials had missed. There was no phobia for electricity among blacks. The new cars had been put in service six months previous; yet the drop in riders began only six weeks ago, following the lynching.

"But the streetcar company had nothing to do with the lynching," the men protested. "It is owned by northern capitalists."

"And run by southern lynchers," Wells shot back. "We have learned that every white man of any standing in town knew of the plan and consented to the lynching of our boys...The colored people feel that every white man in Memphis who consented to his death is as guilty as those who fired the guns which took his life, and they want to get away from this town.

"We told them the week after the lynching to save their nickels and dimes so that they could do so. We had no way of knowing that they were doing so before this," she admitted. She recounted the interview with the officials in the *Free Speech*, to encourage readers to keep up the pressure.[23]

Wells had scolded the Afro-American League the previous summer for not organizing a boycott of separate-car railway lines. Now she discovered how the black exodus hurt white business in a host of ways. Restaurants, clothing stores, and furniture emporiums depended on black business; a number failed. Whole blocks of houses were suddenly up for rent. Women who worked as domestics gave notice, making it difficult for middle-class whites to find help. Music shop owners faced a glut of guitars, pianos, and fiddles as emigrants returned instruments they had been buying on installment plans.[24]

White papers, alert now to the doings of the black community, could not ignore the mass meetings, the exodus, the downturn in business. Some opined that it was "good riddance" to see blacks leave the city, but others were sobered. Stories began appearing that warned of the hardships to be endured in Oklahoma Territory: THE NEW PROMISED LAND, UNLIKE OLD CANAAN, IT DOESN'T FLOW WITH MILK AND HONEY, warned the *Appeal-Avalanche*.[25]

Wells decided to visit Oklahoma and report on conditions herself. For three weeks she toured the territory, visiting settlements founded by African Americans. Langston City had been organized by Edwin P. McCabe, the former state auditor of Kansas, whom she had met on her cross-country trip to California. McCabe's newspaper, the *Langston City Herald*, wrote glowingly of her visit. Wells came away with mixed feelings, however.

Oklahoma did not offer an abundance of working-class jobs, and there seemed to be few advantages for middle-class emigrants, whose capital could provide a base for the new black communities. Despite such discouragements, from four to six thousand African Americans deserted Memphis for the West, more than 5 percent of the city's total population.[26] Wells reported on their progress, encouraged them, but remained stymied over how to address the deteriorating conditions across the South.

❧⸺❧

In the end, she did what she did best: used her intelligence and her "goose quill with diamond point" to bring the condition of black Americans to the attention of the wider world.[27]

In doing so, the Memphis murders forced her to think more deeply about the reports of lynchings that appeared with such depressing regularity. An outsider reading the *Appeal-Avalanche* would have thought that Moss, McDowell, and Stewart were criminal lowlifes, when in fact they were upstanding citizens. When Wells read about other lynchings, she assumed that at least some of the accused—perhaps even the majority—were guilty of the crimes with which they were charged, though of course mob violence had deprived them of a fair trial. Blacks as well as whites, after all, were capable of breaking the law. "Until this past year," she commented in 1893, "I was one among those who believed the condition of the masses gave large excuse for the humiliations and proscriptions under which we labored."[28]

Yet the charge of rape was appearing more and more frequently. What accounted for the rise? Had something changed in the character of Southern black males to make them more aggressive?

Many whites seemed to think so. "The commission of [rape] grows more frequent every year," lamented the all-white *Memphis Commercial* on May 17. "The generation of Negroes which have grown up since the war have lost in large measure the traditional and wholesome awe of the white race which kept the Negroes in subjection…There is no longer a restraint upon the brute passion of the Negro." The *Commercial* referred to three crimes, "equally atrocious," which recently had "happened in quick succession: one in Tennessee, one in Arkansas, and one in Alabama." Even the threat of lynching had not prevented these. "The facts of the crime appear to appeal more to the Negro's lustful imagination than the facts of the punishment do to his fears. He sets aside all fear of death in any form when opportunity is found for the gratification of his bestial desires."[29]

When Wells was in Natchez drumming up subscriptions, one of her hosts pointed out an imposing mansion owned by the Marshalls, a white family that ranked among the city's crème de la crème. A few years earlier, Mrs. Marshall had given birth to a son. His complexion was slightly swarthy, but everyone declared the coloring to be the influence of a brunette forebear. A few years later, however, the second child arrived a definite chocolate brown. In horror, the family groped for explanations: the newborn was dark from "strangulation" or "rush of blood." The doctor disabused them—this was a Negro child. When the news got out, it was found that the Marshalls's black coachman had abruptly packed and left town. When it was discovered that the liaison had been going on for several years, Mrs. Marshall was sent away in disgrace. Her husband, it was said, died within the year of a broken heart.[30]

Wells knew of similar stories in Memphis, of white women who had entered willingly into illicit relationships with black men. There was the wife of a physician who ran away—again, with her coachman. Another woman lived openly with a black man. When threatened with jail for her "crime" of miscegenation, she swore she was black. Lillie Baillie, a young girl, refused to name her black lover when she delivered a dark-skinned baby.[31] Wells recalled her fellow editor, Jesse Duke, who fled in 1887 to Memphis after writing about "the growing appreciation of white Juliets for colored Romeos." The occasion then had been the lynching of another supposed black rapist who, in fact, had been carrying on an affair.

In the newspapers, then, "rape" was not always rape. The charge sometimes masked a relationship based on mutual consent. It also served, Wells began to believe, as a convenient excuse. Even the *Appeal-Avalanche* disapproved of the murders of Moss, McDowell, and Stewart. Lynching was not easy to condone or defend. On the other hand, if the crime being avenged was so heinous, so foul, so beyond the pale of civilized conduct, then such mob action became easier to comprehend. And what crime was more heinous than rape? No less an authority than Methodist bishop Atticus G. Haygood, president of Emory University, explained the point. "No race, not the most savage, tolerates the rape of woman, but it may be said without reflection upon any other people that the Southern people are now and always have been most sensitive concerning the honor of their women—their mothers, wives, sisters, and daughters."[32]

Wells decided to speak out. In the issue of the *Free Speech* for Saturday, May 21—four days after the *Commercial*'s libels about the "Negro's lustful imagination"— she used words that fairly crackled on the page:

> Eight negroes lynched since last issue of the "Free Speech," one at Little Rock, Ark., last Saturday morning where the citizens broke (?) into the penitentiary and got their man; three near Anniston, Ala., one near New Orleans; and three at Clarksville, Ga., the last three for killing a white man, and five on the same old racket—the new alarm about raping white women. The same programme of hanging, then shooting bullets into the lifeless bodies was carried out to the letter.
>
> Nobody in this section of the country believes the old thread bare lie that Negro men rape white women. If Southern white men are not careful, they will over-reach themselves and public sentiment will have a reaction; a conclusion will then be reached which will be very damaging to the moral reputation of their women.[33]

Directly after writing the editorial, Wells left town on a combined vacation and business trip, to attend a conference of the African Methodist Episcopal Church in Philadelphia and then in New York to visit Thomas Fortune, the editor who had done so much to promote her writings. She also wanted to see what the North might be like as a place to live. "Although I had been warned repeatedly by my own people that something would happen if I did not cease harping on the lynching of three months before, I had expected that happening to come when I was at home," she recalled many years later.

The circumstances of May 1892 suggest otherwise. Wells understood the power of her words. In 1891 she had been fired for writing an article critical of the school board. That essay, like her latest, touched on interracial affairs between whites and blacks. That essay, like her latest, went to the press unsigned.

More to the point, she had come to appreciate how white Southerners reacted to any allegation that even hinted that a white woman of moral purity might be attracted to a black man. To suggest such an affinity was to strike sparks to a tinderbox of public rage. And some whites were using that rage deliberately, brandishing the specter of rape as an excuse to intimidate any African American who struck them as too prosperous or outspoken. In the end, Wells acted much as she had when the pursuit of two suitors in love led her to depart for California. Then, Aunt Fannie had written repeatedly before circumstances pushed Ida to leave. This time, friends in Philadelphia "kept writing to say that the conference had been in session two weeks and I must come at once if I hoped to get there before it closed."

Do something. There were no easy choices. In speaking her mind, Wells knew that she risked sharing the fate of Tommie Moss. She said what she had to say—and left town for Philadelphia on Friday, May 20. The *Free Speech* came out on the weekend. By Wednesday, white papers were aflame over the "atrocious paragraph" about "thread bare lies" and "the moral reputation of their women." The *Memphis Scimitar* assumed that the offending author was male, and promptly asserted it the duty of any honorable white man "to tie the wretch who utters these calumnies to a stake at the intersection of Main and Madison Sts., brand him in the forehead with a hot iron and perform upon him a surgical operation with a pair of tailor's shears."[34]

That evening the whites held a meeting at the Cotton Exchange—"not an assemblage of hoodlums or irresponsible fire-eaters, but solid, substantial business men who knew exactly what they were doing," boasted the *Commercial*. The talk hovered around lynching, except Wells was out of town and J. L. Fleming had been warned to flee, barely in time. Taylor Nightingale, the former partner of the *Free Speech*, was found to be back in the city and summoned, struck in the face, and a pistol held to his head until he disavowed the sentiments in the article, along with any part in writing it. A committee then visited the offices of the paper to insure that it never be published again. Creditors repossessed the printing equipment and sold it. Sentinels were posted at the train depots so that if either Wells or Fleming returned, they could be beaten and dumped into the Mississippi River, dead or alive.[35]

The news reached Wells at three in the afternoon, Thursday, May 26. She had just arrived in Jersey City to meet Thomas Fortune after the conclusion of her Philadelphia conference. The dapper editor with wire-rimmed glasses was smiling as he greeted her.

"Well, we've been a long time getting you to New York, but now you are here I am afraid you will have to stay," he said. "From the rumpus you've kicked up I feel assured of it. Oh, I know it was you because it sounded just like you."[36]

Wells professed bewilderment over this welcome.

"Haven't you seen the morning paper?" he asked.

They say. He handed her the *New York Sun*.

· *Eight* ·

EXILED

❧—❧

Sᴜᴄᴄᴇss ᴄᴀᴍᴇ ᴛᴏ Iᴅᴀ Wᴇʟʟs ɪɴ ɢʀᴇᴀᴛᴇʀ ᴍᴇᴀsᴜʀᴇ ᴛʜᴀɴ sʜᴇ could have hoped. Little more than four months after arriving in the North, she sat center stage, fashionably dressed, amidst the gaslights of New York City's Lyric Hall in Manhattan, little more than a block from Madison Square Park.[1] It was Wednesday evening, October 5, 1892. Three months earlier, Ida had celebrated her thirtieth birthday. The guests who arrived—more than two hundred—were among the most distinguished African Americans in the city, in addition to many who had traveled from Boston and Philadelphia. They were shown to their seats by ushers wearing white badges emblazoned with "Iola," the pen name that had spread her fame. Floral arrangements brightened the room, including a "horn of plenty" donated by the ushers themselves. The program promised music and speeches praising Wells's campaign against lynching, but the greatest interest was reserved for the talk to be given by the woman of honor herself.

"We cannot see what the 'good' citizens of Memphis gained by suppressing the *Free Speech*," the *St. Paul Appeal* commented earlier in the summer. "They stopped the papers of a few hundreds subscribers and drove Miss Ida B. Wells to New York, and now she is telling the story to hundreds of thousands of readers." Thomas Fortune had been right about the "rumpus" kicked up. Her paper had been suppressed, while further threats made it clear that she would no longer be safe in Memphis. One member of the business community promised publicly to shoot her if she returned any time in the next twenty years.[2]

Fortune put Wells on salary for weekly articles and offered her a quarter interest in the *New York Age,* in return for the subscriber

IDA B. WELLS.

Wells, ca. 1893–1894

list to the *Free Speech*.[3] So she continued campaigning as before. Yet Wells did more than condemn the epidemic of mob terror. In a long article published June 25, and in others that followed, she laid bare the fraudulent excuse that lynchers were merely acting out a revulsion any decent person might feel for a brutal crime like rape. The *New York Times* had reflected that attitude the previous February, in describing the lynching of Edward Coy, burned to death for raping a white woman in Texarkana, Arkansas. SHE CALLED FOR THE TORCH, ran the headline, assuring New Yorkers that the victim herself had begged to administer vengeance. "A number of citizens deprecate the manner of punishment," the paper noted, "but their number is insignificant compared with the great majority which lends its unqualified indorsement to the deed, insisting and proclaiming loudly that no punishment conceivable was too severe to inflict upon a man whose crime was as shocking and brutal as was the deed of Coy."[4]

Based on her own experience, however, Wells understood that the white press often contained "unreliable and doctored reports of lynchings." While still in Memphis she had begun studying the yearly statistics published by the *Chicago Tribune*. To her surprise, out of 728 mob killings reported from 1882 through 1891, no rape had even been alleged in nearly two-thirds of the cases.[5] Most murders, she pointed out in the *Age,* were committed against blacks who had challenged whites successfully in business, run for political office, refused to be intimidated, or were simply "too sassy." As for the Texarkana case, further investigation revealed that Coy and his supposed victim had been carrying on an affair for more than a year. When news of the liaison leaked out, the leaders of the mob insisted that the woman accuse her lover of rape and then light the match to the bonfire that burned him to death. In his final moments Coy pled with her to reconsider "if she would burn him after they had 'been sweethearting' so long."[6]

The *Times* reporter noted that when a black woman on the scene protested Coy's burning as "cruel," an "old white-haired negro" was said to have reproved her. "What did you say, niggah? Ain't you got no sense?…If he was to do to my wife or my gal like he did dat white woman, you better bleebe I'd burn de black rascal too."[7] Such commentary, Wells recognized, was meant to encourage just that sort of "understanding" attitude among both blacks and whites. "What would you do if your wife or daughter were so assaulted?" asked Bishop Oscar Fitzgerald, of the Methodist Church South, when asked if he would condemn lynching. Indeed, even the grand old foe of slavery, Frederick Douglass, confessed to Wells that her exposé was "a revelation." He "had been troubled by the increasing number of lynchings," she recalled, "and had begun to believe it true that there was increasing lasciviousness on the part of Negroes."[8]

The June 25 article was a bombshell and Fortune knew it. He printed ten thousand copies of his paper and sent them throughout the South, as well as to regular subscribers. A thousand were sold in Memphis alone.[9] When more requests for the exposé came in, two respected black women from the city proposed organizing a program, both to honor Wells for her efforts and to raise money so that her articles could appear in a pamphlet entitled *Southern Horrors*. As word of the event spread and interest rose, the gala was moved to Lyric Hall.

On stage Wells was flanked by a row of distinguished black women older than she. From Boston came Josephine St. Pierre

Ruffin, an activist who had organized aid for emigrants to Kansas at the end of Reconstruction and who now spoke in favor of women's suffrage. Mrs. Gertrude Mossell of Philadelphia, another black journalist who had written for Thomas Fortune, came to praise her younger colleague. New York City's most distinguished black female physician, Susan McKinney, also was present, as was Sarah Garnet, the widow of black abolitionist Henry Highland Garnet.

As Wells looked out over the audience, she was gratified by the show of support. Could she have anticipated that the words of protest she was about to deliver would become a central part of her life in the years to come? Perhaps not, but within a year she surely began to believe it might be so. During the coming winter of 1892–1893 the New York lecture would be repeated in Pennsylvania, Delaware, and Washington D.C. Meanwhile Josephine Ruffin coordinated a New England tour through Rhode Island and Massachusetts, including at least three visits to that mecca of abolition and reform, Boston.

Wells's third lecture there, in February 1893, gave hope that her message was getting through. For the first time she spoke to a white audience—to those who possessed political power and who had long tended to ignore lynchings because the crime of rape seemed so outrageous. Even progressive whites held meetings like the "Mohonk Conference on the Negro Question," debating earnestly how to reduce the crime rate of African Americans, rather than how to reduce the mob violence perpetrated against them. Nobody was much interested discussing "the White question." As one speaker at Mohonk concluded, "Ultimately, in the homes of the colored people the problem of the colored race will be settled."[10] Although Wells's Boston talk was reported by the city's

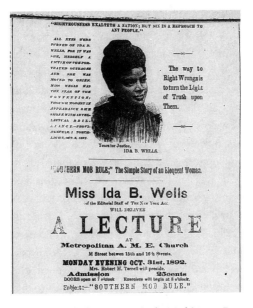

Detail from an advertisement in the Washington Bee, *October 22, 1892, for a lecture*

major papers, it did not provide the needed breakthrough to a broader American audience. If anything, the lesson of her tours seemed to be that most white Northerners were no more determined to stop lynchings than most white Southerners.

The key to amplifying Wells's appeal lay across the Atlantic. The American press began to pay attention only after an English Quaker, Catherine Impey, persuaded Ida to lecture in Great Britain. She made two extended visits, giving some twenty talks in 1893 and more than a hundred in 1894, occasionally to audiences of more than a thousand.[11] Wells's pamphlet *Southern Horrors* preceded her, but it was her personal appearance and her demeanor that made listeners take note:

> Miss Ida B. Wells is a negress, a young lady of little more than twenty years of age, a graceful, sweet-faced, intelligent, courageous girl. She hails from Memphis, Tenn. She is not going back there just now, because the white people are anxious to hang her up by the neck in the market place and burn the soles of her feet, and gouge her beautiful dark eyes out with red-hot irons. This is what the Southern American white man does with a negro or negress for preference, when he wants a holiday sensation; and when he finds a charming victim, such as this sweet girl would make, the mayor of the town orders the schools to be closed, and the parents don their Sunday-go-to-meeting best, and lead the youngsters out by the hand. They all go out to see the fun, and have their photographs taken at the scene of the martyrdom, and there is much rejoicing over the black sinner that repenteth not.

They say—once again in the *Memphis Appeal-Avalanche*, but this time the paper was quoting the *London Sun*.[12] The Memphis papers did not much care for this English version of Wells. They preferred their own characterizations: notorious negro courtesan, disreputable colored woman, saddle-colored Sapphira, intriguing adventuress, strumpet, malicious wanton, infamous slanderer and traducer.[13]

More to the point, Wells made sure that it was not just Southern papers that noticed her tour. During her stay in London, where she spoke on thirty-five different occasions, she and her British hosts scoured the daily papers in search of the fullest coverage of each lecture, and then bought at least a hundred copies. As Wells recalled, "The next morning's work was to gather around the table in the breakfast room and mark and address those newspapers." Copies went out to prominent ministers, senators, governors, major American papers, and the president of the United States, to keep Americans "informed as to the progress of the 'Negro adventuress and her movements.' "[14]

Both how much Wells would accomplish over the coming decades—and how little, given the immense obstacles facing her—she could not have guessed that evening in Lyric Hall. She had no illusions that the battle would be short or easy. Sometimes the latest news seemed to outdo itself in shades of horror. The school-closing "holiday sensation," which the *London Sun* indirectly referred to, involved a lynching in Paris, Texas, described by Wells in her updated lecture. The "mob" in Paris was not eight or ten men hidden by masks and the dark of night, but a daylight crowd ten thousand strong, the size of an entire town, which had gathered from as far away as Dallas and Forth Worth, a hundred miles distant, in response to newspaper accounts of the preparations for public torture and execution. Other dispatches continued to come in during the tours. After a lecture in Manchester, one of Wells's listeners read aloud an account of a black woman in San Antonio, Texas, shut up in a barrel into which nails were driven. She was rolled down a hill until she was dead.[15] In Memphis, a new lynching had taken place, planned well enough in advance that a telegram could be sent, taunting Wells by inviting her to come cover the event.[16]

Despite such atrocities, the lectures in Britain made a difference in the way both Northerners and Southerners in the United States perceived lynching. Papers such as the *New York Times*, though still suspicious of "the mulatress missionary," began to treat lynchings with more evident disapproval.[17]

Their coverage of Wells increased too, some of it favorable. In addition, leading clergy in England signed a testimonial, begging their American counterparts to let Wells speak at home. Possessed of this entering wedge, she convinced more than a few white ministers to let her speak. She spent much of the following year campaigning across the nation from east to west. Southern states, of course, were too dangerous to visit, and border states proved unfruitful. ("In St. Louis, the sentiment was too strongly southern.")[18]

Still, white citizens of Memphis were chastened by Wells's attacks. In 1895, when six black men were murdered there after being accused of burning a barn, a public meeting at the Merchant's Exchange condemned the "wicked, fiendish and inexcusable massacre." The same newspapers that had called Wells an adventuress concurred. A reward was raised for assistance in capturing the conspirators, as well as a fund to compensate the widows of the victims. Thirteen whites were indicted, although the papers' newfound outrage carried little weight with the jury. It acquitted all of the defendants.[19] Lynching would continue across the South as well as elsewhere in the nation, though never again so frequently as in 1892 and 1893. Wells labored doggedly—often to the point of exhaustion—to protest, lead, and shame her fellow citizens into action.

❧—❧

Do something. Until her death in 1931 at the age of sixty-nine, Wells never ceased confronting the obstacles facing African Americans. The power of the pen remained central to her efforts. Over the course of several years, she held the editorships of two newspapers, the *Conservator* and the *Fellowship Herald*. She continued to publish pamphlets and articles on lynching. *Southern Horrors* (1892) was followed by *A Red Record* (1895), *Lynch Law in Georgia* (1899), *Mob Rule in New Orleans* (1900), *Lynch Law in America* (1900), "How Enfranchisement Stops Lynching" (1910), "Our Country's Lynching Record" (1913), *The East St. Louis Massacre: The Greatest Outrage of the Century* (1917), and *The Arkansas Race Riot* (1920), among others. Whenever possible Wells sought to visit the site of a supposed "outrage," to discredit the distorted accounts that usually appeared.

As a former teacher, Wells believed that setting youth on the right path was key to overcoming poverty and racism. In Chicago, where she eventually settled and in 1895 married a distinguished black lawyer and activist, Ferdinand L. Barnett, she helped launch a neighborhood kindergarten at a time when the idea was relatively new. After her own four children had all begun elementary school, Wells established a storefront reading room and social center, much like Jane Addams's settlement houses. At the center, located in a rough neighborhood along Chicago's State Street, African Americans could find leads to a job, a meal or a bed, or just a quiet place to read. Three years later, Wells took a full-time job as Chicago's first black probation officer.

She would never stop looking to organize or to leverage power through clubs and federations, at a time when the organizational impulse for both men and women was sweeping the country. Professional societies in law, medicine, and the social sciences as well as the nationwide Federated Women's Clubs were a few among many groups springing up to address the problems of licensing, of professional standards, and of the ills of the new urban industrial world.

In Memphis, as race relations worsened, Wells had hailed the Mutual Protective Association. About the same time, she encouraged Thomas Fortune's National Afro-American League. Decade after decade she joined—or helped to found, campaigned for, or prodded into taking stronger action—the National Association of Colored Women, the Anti-Lynching Society of London, the Prison Congress of the United States, the Ida B. Wells Club (named in her honor), the Afro-American Historical Society, the National Association for the Advancement of Colored People (NAACP), the Negro Fellowship League, the National Equal Rights Movement, the Illinois Equal Suffrage Association, and the Alpha Suffrage Club. After World War I, Marcus Garvey's Universal Negro Improvement Association chose her to attend the Versailles peace conference on its behalf, though the government refused permission to such "agitators" to travel abroad. In Chicago, Wells joined the Women's Forum, the Third Ward Women's Political Club, and the Anthropological Society, a group promoting interracial tolerance. Two months before her death, she joined the United Clubs Emergency Relief movement, to help alleviate the human toll of the Great Depression.

Amid the continual flurry of "agitating, investigating and publishing facts and figures in the lynching evil," Wells was often disappointed by those same organizations.[20] They were not pressing hard enough, she complained. More than once she withdrew when her talents or views went unused or unappreciated. She made enemies among those who might have been her allies. Over the years, she parted ways with Thomas Fortune and with her friend Meb Britton, the latter having criticized her antilynching campaign.[21] (Did Britton also resent Wells's condemnation of interracial affairs shortly before Hattie Britton's suicide?) At first the National Association of

Wells during World War I. She is wearing a button she designed to protest the execution of eleven black soldiers in 1917 following a riot.

Colored Women received Wells's support, but she fell out with its president, her acquaintance Mollie Church Terrell. Wells was often at loggerheads with leaders of the NAACP, whom she believed were slow to pursue black civil rights. She even broke briefly with Frederick Douglass in 1893, when the Columbian World's Exposition refused to include a building dedicated to black culture and history. Douglass accepted the proposed alternative of a "Colored American Day," whereas Wells decried the idea as a demeaning "half a loaf." When the event succeeded despite her fears, she admitted she had been a "hothead" and apologized.[22]

Some observers attributed Wells's stubborn streak to zeal for her cause, to personal temperament, or even to a desire for the spotlight. "She was a great fighter," recalled Mary White Ovington, a white founder of the NAACP, "but we knew she had to play a lone hand. And if you have too many players of lone hands in your organization, you soon have no game." The *Chicago Inter-Ocean,* a paper Wells relied on and supported, commented, "Miss Wells has the weakness of most agitators who lose sight of everything but the cause they advocate, and misunderstand those not willing to blindly follow them."[23]

Ida did recognize her own thin skin. "Temper…has always been my besetting sin," she conceded, and she prayed often for self-control. "O My Father, forgive me, forgive me & take away the remembrance of those hateful words, uttered for the satisfaction of self…Father help me, I pray be more thoughtful & considerate in speech…O help me to better control my temper."[24]

But the quarrels with black organizations grew out of more than impatience and egotism. African Americans at the turn of the century faced an immensely frustrating environment in which racism was by turns casual, malicious, unthinking, and brutal. Often there seemed no clear course of action that would produce progress on civil rights. Put up with casual slurs in hopes of "getting along" in white society? So often, the result seemed only to compromise one's dignity day after day. Demand civil rights boldly? To do so risked white retaliation by lynching or even through riots that destroyed entire neighborhoods. More than once, Wells made common cause with suffrage advocate Susan B. Anthony, who strongly supported her stand on racial equality. Still, Anthony's prime object was the vote for women.

She recognized that to reach her goal, at least some Southern states would have to ratify the proposed constitutional amendment. White Southern suffragists refused to accept black supporters in their delegations, and Anthony was willing to bend, to put up with some segregation, for the sake of results. Wells was not.[25]

Even more frustrating to Wells was Booker T. Washington's accommodating position on civil rights. Washington prided himself on his realism. In a speech at the Atlanta Cotton States Exhibition in 1895 he famously laid out what he saw as a practical way for African Americans to get along with whites in the new, more strictly segregated South. His "Atlanta Compromise" proposed that blacks voluntarily give up any role in politics and devote themselves instead to economic progress through hard work. As more blacks prospered, whites would see the advantage of granting them a greater role in American life. Many African Americans came to agree with Washington's stand, especially after white leaders praised him for his wisdom.

Wells could no longer accept what had once been her "honest conviction," that "maintenance of character, money getting and education would finally solve our problem, and that it depended on us to say how soon this would be brought about."[26] Her own investigations suggested that it was precisely "getting ahead" that provoked lynching. As she put it succinctly in 1909:

First: Lynching is color line murder.
Second: Crime against women is the excuse, not the cause.
Third: It is a national crime and requires a national remedy.[27]

If lynching was directed at keeping African Americans behind a color line, in inferior positions, Booker T. Washington's call for accommodation was largely useless. If success could come only with a national remedy (and not merely a Southern one), then Susan Anthony's urge to compromise on segregation to pass woman suffrage was also wishful thinking. What use was it to compromise if all it did was give racist white women the vote? Segregation and lynching had to be approached head-on, not indirectly or through compromise. Half a century later, Martin Luther King would write from a jail cell in Birmingham that there was always someone ready to counsel "Wait!" for a more appropriate time. But the call to "wait," King argued, almost always meant "never."[28]

Time and again Wells was proved right when she warned that patience and hard work alone could not yield results. The soothing words of the Atlanta Compromise did not prevent a race riot from breaking out in that city little more than a decade later, during which white mobs attacked African Americans and destroyed their property. Nor did patience prevent similar riots in Springfield, Illinois (1908) or East St. Louis and Houston (1917) or Chicago and Philips County, Arkansas (1919) or in Tulsa, Oklahoma (1921). Before being executed on the outskirts of Memphis, Tom Moss had advised his people to go West. In 1911, however, the photographer G. H. Farnum was selling picture postcards of the lynching from the Canadian River bridge in Okemah, Oklahoma.[29] Had Laura Nelson, lynched there along with her son, been among the thousands of families who had moved out of Memphis, looking for greater freedom? The newspapers did not say.

Wells kept speaking out, joining organizations, holding the world to her high standards. In later decades, though, her focus increasingly became local. People began to forget the work she had done in Britain and across the nation. When the NAACP convened a National Conference on Lynching in 1919, Wells chose not to come. When the National Equal Rights League organized a similar meeting in 1930, she was not there. And in 1922, when black scholar Carter G. Woodson published his study of African Americans, *The Negro in Our History*, the name of Ida B. Wells was nowhere to be found.

In her heyday, the black press praised Wells as the Joan of Arc of her people. Late in life she was approached by a young woman, who told her of a YWCA vesper service at which Joan of Arc had been the topic. Each worshiper had been asked to name someone possessing Saint Joan's legendary qualities. This young woman, the only African American at the meeting, named Mrs. Ida B. Wells-Barnett. No one else there had any idea why the comparison should be made—even the young woman who made it. "Mrs. Barnett, I couldn't tell why I thought so. I have heard you mentioned so often by that name, so I gave it. I was dreadfully embarrassed. Won't you please tell me what it was you did, so the next time I am asked…I can give an intelligent answer?"[30]

In October 1892, Wells knew nothing of this future, neither the question from the young woman, nor her own sense of dismay upon hearing it, nor her characteristic response—to write an autobiography (nearly complete at the time of her death), which one day would spark a renewed appreciation of her role in the antilynching campaign. As Wells rose to take the lectern at Lyric Hall, she had only her past, the words of her speech, and perhaps a silent prayer.

"Let my work prosper in Thy Hands my Father & let me not trust in myself, nor forget the lessons of humility Thou hast taught."[31]

She did not trust herself to lecture off the cuff. Although her elocution lessons and recitations of *Macbeth* stood her in good stead, she had always memorized those efforts. While she appreciated the melodrama in "'Ostler Joe" and other Victorian creations, her own speeches remained direct, logical, and devoid "of all oratorical tricks," as one English journalist observed. Another noted her "singular refinement, dignity and self-restraint," adding that he had never "met any 'agitator' so cautious and unimpassioned in speech."[32] Wells understood that if she hoped to be believed by white audiences as well as black, she could not appear overwrought or, worse still, "hysterical," lest her emotions be taken as a sign of "women's weakness" and her arguments discounted. She prided herself at not breaking down in a public lecture.

"Born and reared in the South, I had never expected to live elsewhere." So she told her listeners in Lyric Hall. In the *New York Age*, she had sometimes recounted the experiences of her race in general terms, like a lawyer reviewing her case. Yet the narrative was always intensely personal, could only be intensely personal, for it was her life and her past as she knew it when she spoke of the Afro-American receiving "freedom, the ballot box, and the Civil Rights Law." As a young girl, she had listened with pride when her father reported Union League parades a mile long in Holly Springs. With the rest of her family, she had endured the forged "red tiger" ballots and other frauds, as Democrats wrested control from the majority in Marshall County and installed the head of the Ku Klux Klan as county sheriff. When she spoke of the new "separate car laws," it had been her own humiliation when the train conductor forced her, unladylike, to disembark at the next station.[33] When she reminded her audience of the numberless times that "the race has been indicted for ignorance, immorality and general worthlessness," those instances included the many whispers that Ida Wells was a harlot, that she took money from white men for sex, that the young sister that she was raising was an illegitimate daughter, that she was fired from her teaching job for immorality.[34]

As she began to relate to her audience the details of the lynchings of Moss, McDowell, and Stewart, she was taken back in her mind's eye to Memphis, the city that had so long been a part of her life despite all the indignities and slights: nights at the theater enjoyed with friends; the latest wares sampled at Menken's; horseback rides; socials and soirées; church services. It was a life she had now been defined out of: *They say*. "A feeling of loneliness and homesickness for the days and the friends that were gone came over me and I felt the tears coming," she recalled:

A panic seized me. I was afraid that I was going to make a scene and spoil all [that] those dear good women had done for me. I kept saying to myself that whatever happened I must not break down, and so I kept on reading. I had left my handkerchief on the seat behind me and therefore could not wipe away the tears which were coursing down my cheeks. The women were all back of me on the platform and could not see my plight. Nothing in my voice, it seemed, gave them an inkling of the true state of affairs. Only those in the audience could see the tears dropping. At last I put my hand behind me and beckoned even as I kept reading. Mrs. Matthews, the chairman, came forward and I asked her for my handkerchief. She brought it and I wiped my nose and streaming face, but I kept on reading the story which they had come to hear.[35]

In a display of pride, the organizing committee had arranged a series of gas jets on stage, spelling out "Iola" in large letters. In truth, after arriving in New York Wells had begun to use another pen name, "Exiled." She chose it with an air of defiance, perhaps even a touch of bravado. Still, she felt her fate keenly. "I had hoped such great things…for my people generally," she wrote after her railroad suit had been rejected. "Just now if it were possible [I] would gather my race in my arms and fly far away with them. O God is there no redress, no peace, no justice in this land for us?"[36]

Ida Wells, thirty years old, dressed finely and surrounded by those who had come to praise her, read the words she had written in longhand, and wept.

Afterword

❧——❧

"Y ES, BUT DO YOU *LIKE* IDA WELLS?" ASKED A FRIEND AND FELLOW historian. She had read a fair amount of Wells's writings, including her diary from the 1880s, and had noticed the mercurial temperament. I was about halfway through the writing of this book when my friend put the question to me. I was a bit startled to realize that I hadn't asked it myself. I found Wells fascinating. I had never stopped to consider whether I liked her.

Perhaps the oversight arose because I was not thinking of *'They Say'* as a biography. It ends, after all, when Wells is thirty, just approaching the apogee of her career. More than half of her very active life remained to be lived. In any case, two studies of Wells have appeared within the past ten years that sensitively explore her contributions over a full lifetime. Although the subtitle of *'They Say'* is *Ida B. Wells and the Reconstruction of Race,* the more I wrote, the more I became convinced that the reconstruction of "race" was the book's central focus.

In that regard, lynching—not Wells—had been my point of entry to the story. In 2001 I read, or tried to read, *Without Sanctuary: Lynching Photography in America*. The hangings,

burnings, and executions depicted within were extremely difficult to look at. James Allen, who collected the photographs, noted
that for him, they provoked "a strong sense of denial...and a
desire to freeze my emotions." What shocked me as much as the
acts of torture themselves was their memorialization on postcards. I had grown up having been introduced to the garden-
variety, rosy-tinted reproductions, collected by my strange and
imperious great aunt Robina, who fled the winters of Rochester,
N.Y., for Miami and brought back the beaches and palm trees
to be stowed in a cubbyhole in her secretary. *Without Sanctuary*
possessed a few such tinted wonders, including a quaint view of
Cairo, Illinois, with trolley car and a decorative archway stretched
across Commercial Street. That one, however, also included a
handwritten x by the arch and the notation, "where they hung
the coon." Most of the cards were more explicit, like the photo of
Laura Nelson seen in the prologue of this book, peddled to Allen
by a flea-market trader who pulled him aside and "in conspirato-
rial tones" offered to sell him a *real* photo postcard.[1]

What struck me—clearly it struck Allen too—was the
demeanor of the observers, and the notion that in the cultural
landscape of the period lynching seemed normal enough that
many whites were unconcerned about appearing in the reproductions—in many cases, were eager to. They did not worry, as
the writers of the family postcards shown in the prologue did,
whether their appearance seemed "natchel" or unnatural. ("This
is the barbecue we had last night," read the message on a card featuring one particularly gruesome burning, "my picture is to the
left with a cross over it your son Joe").[2] Reproducing the photos
as postcards, buying and sending them: these were all acts of

definition—definition of others and definition of self. That was what interested and unsettled me.

In constructing a narrative, then, I wanted the first approach to be from the skewed perspective that I suspected many readers shared with me, where it took only a slow drift around a bend in the Canadian River to transform picturesque nostalgia into much more troubling markers of identity. James Baldwin's aphorism came to mind. "If I am not who you say I am, then you are not who you think you are." Baldwin's actual words were more explicit than the paraphrase regularly attributed to him. He spoke to teachers in 1963 on the subject of "The Negro Child—His Self-Image." "So where we are now," he concluded, "is that a whole country of people believe I'm a 'nigger,' and I don't, and the battle's on! Because if I am not what I've been told I am, then it means that you're not what you thought you were either! And that is the crisis."[3] At the end of the nineteenth century, as much as in Baldwin's twentieth, African Americans and whites were defining their relations with one another in starkly different ways. As was so often the case in American history, race seemed to be at the center of the cultural misperceptions.

❧—❧

In Wells's post-emancipation South, race meant everything and nothing. Nothing, in the sense that Haiti's twentieth-century dictator "Papa Doc" Duvalier indicated, when he answered a journalist's question about what percentage of Haiti's population was white. "Ninety-eight," Duvalier is said to have replied. The American reporter blinked. Surely the ruler of one of the blackest nations in the hemisphere had misunderstood. No, 98 percent, Duvalier insisted. "How do you define white?" queried the baffled reporter. "How do you define black in your country?" countered Duvalier. When the journalist responded that a person with any black blood was considered black, Duvalier nodded. "Well, that's the way we define white in my country."[4] Geneticists have established the scientific futility of trying to define race, be it black, white, red, or brown. Differences within supposed racial groups are hugely greater than any genetic differences among them.[5] Race is a fictional, scientifically meaningless construct.

In her own day, Wells was very much aware of the evolving standard of race—the "invisible drop," as she called it. This was the dictum Duvalier alluded to, that anyone with even a single drop of black blood was black.[6] She also recognized the racism embedded in this asymmetry. Why not refer to Wells as "white," if just one drop was enough to tip the balance one way or another? Further, the asymmetry passed from one generation to the next. A "white" woman could give birth to a "black" baby (usually to the consternation of her family); but the possibility was never conceded that a "black" woman could bear a "white" child, no matter how light the baby's skin.

For of course race meant everything in post-emancipation America. Even if it was a social construct, a fiction based on no scientific evidence, race served to define lives to such a degree that it would have been delusional for Wells to describe herself as white.[7] She identified with her race and proudly spoke of her father Jim Wells as a "race man." She condemned well-to-do blacks who shrank from acknowledging any bond with other African Americans. She would have agreed with anthropologist W. O. Brown who remarked in 1931, the year of her death, that "the race conscious posit their race as an entity to which they must have obligations. They have a conscience about this race. They must serve it, fight for it, be loyal to it. To the outsider, the race of the race conscious may appear to be an imaginative construction, but to the initiated, the race is a reality, in a sense, a personal experience."[8]

Precisely because race was a social construction, however, it was fluid. It had no fixed nature, but evolved and changed. Its definition depended on who was doing the constructing. During the decades in which Ida Wells came of age, a continuing struggle of definition and self-definition accorded race increasing importance. The struggle arose out of the vacuum created when emancipation eliminated the legal categories of *slave* and *free*. If the law of the land prescribed a status, *slave*, which could be upheld and regulated, race was a useful concept but not necessarily paramount. Once the legal props of slavery disappeared, however, it became much more difficult for one group of people to justify keeping another in an inferior position. Race was the key. A line was drawn—the color line, as Wells called it—that during the 1880s and 1890s was increasingly buttressed by new laws, customs, and sanctions, until that single drop of "black blood" was sufficient to make the line sharp, bright, and unyielding.

One brilliant study that has explored the progression from slavery to race is Martha Hodes's *White Women, Black Men: Illicit Sex in the Nineteenth-Century South* (1997). Like Wells, Hodes recognized that the relation between white women and black men deserved particular attention. Under slave law, bondage was matrilineal: the child of a black woman was always deemed to be a slave, regardless of the father's race, while the child of a white woman and black father was deemed to be free. Under such a system, sexual relations between white men and black women were tolerated, for the offspring did not threaten the institution of slavery. Somewhat surprisingly, Hodes found that before emancipation, even illicit sex between white women and black men was often endured, so long as the affair remained childless. Only when a free white woman gave birth to a free black child did both custom and the courts act more harshly.

Lynching, however, played no significant role under the regime of slavery, for the simple reason that a black slave remained some-one's property. Only following emancipation did mob violence become more common. As one Northerner noted shortly after the war, "The pecuniary value which the individual negro for-merly represented having disappeared, the maiming and killing of colored men seems to be looked upon by many as one of those venial offences which must be forgiven to the outraged feelings of a wronged and robbed people." As Hodes succinctly concluded:

> Political power, economic success, and sex with a white woman— all such actions on the part of a black man confounded the lines of racial categories in a South without slavery, and therefore became unforgivable transgressions in the eyes of whites. Without the legal status of slavery and freedom as a dividing line, white Southerners had to rely on the fickle categories of "black" and "white" to define white supremacy. The color line, therefore, had to be fixed in two ways. It had to be established first by stricter racial definitions, which would come to fruition in the late nineteenth century with a codified "one-drop rule." It also had to be established by distinct political, economic, and social castes for white men and black men, a task that required constant vigilance on the part of white people in order to ensure that no black man crossed over into the territory of political power, economic independence, or social authority.[9]

Hodes also could have added that constant efforts were required on the part of black men and women to resist or come to terms with this growing system of segregation.

It was this struggle for self-definition on the part of African Americans that struck me as worth exploring. I preferred narrative to analysis, however, as a way to convey the flavor as well as the substance of that day-to-day battle. Here, Wells seemed an inspired subject. As an outspoken critic of lynching, she placed herself at the center of black efforts to resist the emerging caste system based on race. Yet even before she became a self-conscious advocate, she provided a vivid example of a black woman— intelligent, attractive, determined—seeking to carve out a life as a member of the middle class. Her diary from the mid-1880s in particular offered a remarkable window into her daily efforts to earn a living, to partake fully of the emerging consumer culture, to engage in the intellectual life of Victorian America, and to find a husband who would love her and respect her talents. I saw Wells not so much as a biographical subject but as a marvelous exemplar of what African American women and men across the South were attempting to accomplish in a society that had newly promised freedom.

In one sense, of course, Wells was not at all typical of most African Americans in the late nineteenth century. The Victorian values she shared were a part of a world far removed from that of the vast majority of Southern blacks, propertyless former slaves who became sharecroppers and tenant farmers, who toiled from day to day, season to season, year to year, planting, cultivating, and harvesting their crops with little or no compensation, and often growing deeper and deeper in debt as they did. The emerging black middle class of which Wells was a part was very small, indeed tiny in comparison those larger numbers. As an exemplar, Wells was if anything in advance of her time.

Yet in the larger scheme of things, she was not in advance of her people's aspirations. The tremendous outpouring of a desire for education after the war, manifested in so many black communities across the South, both urban and rural, revealed where hope lay. And the serendipity of Wells's birth date, aligning so nearly with Lincoln's Emancipation Proclamation, meant that the first thirty years of her life would cover those first thirty years of freedom after slavery, and chart one of the most tenacious pursuers of those hopes.

It also meant, however, that the most difficult narrative to reconstruct would be of Reconstruction itself, when Wells was only a child and her surviving memories few. Wells's autobiography devoted only half a dozen pages to those years. Clearly her parents played a large role in shaping her attitudes, both in the public spaces of Holly Springs, where Jim Wells stood up to his employer and opened up for business after he had been fired; and in the private spaces of the home, where Lizzie Wells was a demanding mother who instilled a strict moral and religious code.

Public spaces, of course, provided the stage upon which definition and self-definition competed: between what *they say* and what *I say*. I was struck by the frequency and diversity of "sidewalk encounters," not only in the months and years immediately following the Civil War, but also as a phenomenon recurring decade after decade, in which whites and blacks measured and recalibrated attitudes. Given that the perceptions of what happened during those encounters diverged so radically, it is almost impossible to determine after the fact whether whites, in one case or another, were actually forced into the street (almost surely they were in some cases, especially by black soldiers who as slaves had been forced to give way for so long); or whether blacks were merely determined to share the walk, which to sensitive whites seemed highly aggressive conduct.

The hypersensitivity of many whites, brought on by the new status of the freedmen, had extreme consequences. Those could be seen in a congressional investigation of one lynching during Reconstruction. "Let me understand the character of the allegation," asked a member of Congress. "You say that he made some insulting proposal to a white lady?" "O, no," the witness replied, "…he had just made some insulting remark. He remarked, 'How d'ye, sis,' or something of that kind, as the young lady passed down the road.'" In the early 1880s, Ferdinand Barnett, the attorney Wells would one day marry, made a similar observation after a black man was lynched for an attempted "outrage." "An attempt, mind you. This is a comprehensive term in the South. It embraces a wink by a colored man at a white girl a half mile off."[10]

Forty years after the event, whites in Holly Springs remembered the sidewalk jostling of rival schools as their students were escorted home at the end of the day. In the 1880s, Wells was still recording incidents of whites who would not give way. In the 1930s, Farm Service Administration photographer Marion Wolcott captured just such an encounter, in which a white woman with her baby is being passed on the walk by three African Americans.

The body language speaks volumes. All three men are in motion, as the angles of their legs reveal. The woman's feet, however, are squarely planted. She holds on tightly to her baby. For her, a crowded

sidewalk is no casual encounter. The man just passing recognizes the tension too: his head is turned to look at the woman as he passes.

Public spaces were contested territory all the way into the civil rights era of the 1960s. The same discomfort is nicely evoked (in a companion book in this series) by a white historian, James E. Crisp, recalling his Texas boyhood. As a teenager growing up in a small town, Crisp considered himself a liberal and a supporter of civil rights. Still, he had scant personal contact with African Americans until a trip in 1960 to an integrated swimming pool in nearby Denton. "I bounced high off the springboard, dove deep into the water, and surfaced midway down the pool, shaking the water off my face. When I opened my eyes again, I found myself only about nine inches from a young black man who was also enjoying the pool. I knew that something was wrong. I couldn't breathe properly, I was getting dizzy, and I knew that I had to get out of the pool...I had an inexplicable, visceral feeling that one of us should not be there."[11]

Sidewalk encounters, to be sure, were only one small aspect of the broader process of definition and self-definition. Painters have a term of their craft, "negative space," which they find useful in learning to render a figure. One pays attention not only to an object, but to the shapes enclosed by it; not only to the bend of an arm when a hand is placed on a hip, but to the shape of the inner triangle bounded by ribs, elbow, and limb. Observing the negative space helps delineate the positive subject.

In the case of Wells's childhood, where little information about her family has survived, white recollections from Holly Springs provide useful negative boundaries of a positive space. The recollections were incorporated into a history of Reconstruction in Marshall County published by the Mississippi Historical Society in 1912. These accounts were negative in a double sense, having been compiled by a white Southerner, Ruth Watkins, during the height of white supremacy.

Although the façade of Watkins's narrative was staid and proper, the tone betrayed her sympathies at every turn. In describing an attack of white Democrats on a Republican rally in Holly Springs, she seemed to suggest that the Klansman George Myers led it almost against his will. Outraged by a supposed "false statement" made by Republican Nelson Gill, Colonel Myers, "without any thought of consequences, jumped on the platform and declared it to be a lie, and struck Gill." Myers was not really the aggressor, merely a wronged Southern gentleman defending his honor. Watkins ended her account with "an amusing incident" wherein a future district attorney for the county "looked around for a weapon with which to defend himself ["defend"—the mob instigated the attack!]. He seized upon the wooden leg of a negro, who was on the platform, and was making desperate efforts to unbuckle it when order was restored." Watkins's hostility emerged even in glancing ways, as when she referred to the black migration to Kansas in 1878 as "the great negro hegira" rather than as an "exodus," the term used by African Americans.[12] A biblical metaphor would have dignified the movement. Watkins preferred an Islamic term, surely perceived by her readers as more derogatory.

Yet by using such negative spaces to delineate positive objects, a historian can transfigure the scenes so disdainfully depicted— "obscene" torchlight rallies, "offensive" mile-long parades—to reveal the sometimes heady world of the Union League in the late 1860s and early 1870s. Meaning to disparage, Watkins nevertheless portrayed a black community gathering by the hundreds, as well as strengthening county government and building up an infrastructure of public services. Such details make clear the excitement and hope Jim Wells shared with Ida as she grew up in Holly Springs.

❦

In the spaces of private life, there was much to be discovered too. The missionary schoolteachers of Shaw University no doubt helped instill in Ida the values of Victorian America but her mother's influence was even more vital. The devotion of Lizzie Wells to her family radiated through her heartfelt religious instruction, the high standards she lay down for her children, her insistence on immaculate housekeeping, and a commitment to education. If anything, the lack of easy access to middle-class culture made the dedication to these standards more intense, especially in Holly Springs, which prided itself on its refinement. Yet those sources of self-definition, standing in positive relief, must be supplemented by the spaces in Wells's autobiographical narrative that seem empty but in truth speak loudly through their silence.

One such space lies just beyond the whipping that Peggy, Ida's grandmother, received the day after her white master died. Significantly, the memory was one of the few Wells retained of her childhood, her ears "burning" to understand why the white mistress punished her grandmother, but understanding that she was too young ask why her father refused to visit his former white mistress. Wells's autobiography maintained a curious distance in explaining the significance of the whipping. "Since I have grown old enough to understand I cannot help but feel what an insight to slavery [my father's words] give," she wrote, without overtly discussing the illicit relationship of which her grandmother had been a part. Mollie Church grew up about the same time in Memphis and used similarly indirect language in her autobiography. Her father took her on Sundays to see "Captain Church" without ever quite explaining who this white steamboat owner was. "Captain Church is certainly good to us, Papa," Mollie remarked at the age of four or five, after receiving yet another gift of flowers or fruit. "'And don't you know, Papa, you look just like

Captain Church. I reckon you look like him because he likes you,'
I added, trying to explain in my childish way the striking resemblance between the two men. Then my father explained the relationship existing between Captain Church and himself."[13] Which
was to say, father and son, but even as an older woman Mollie
Church could not bring herself to be so explicit on the page! In a
Victorian world that emphasized sexual propriety, discussion of
such matters would always remain slightly shameful, especially
when the white press so often defined black women as sexually
lax. Once again, there was an asymmetry in this construction of
race. Black women were seen as wanton when they participated
in such liaisons, even if forced; white men were guilty only of
indiscretion.

Thus when Ida Wells came to Memphis around 1881, she had
already absorbed the values of a middle-class Victorian woman.
While those values were attributed, first and foremost, to the
proper virtues of Britain's Queen Victoria, as a cultural system
Victorianism responded more to the threats and instabilities of
the emerging industrial age. During an era in which "dark Satanic
mills" made and unmade the lives and fortunes of struggling
workers, middle-class clerks, the nouveau riche as well as down-
at-the-heels landed gentry, Victorian values of "refinement" and
"manners" established a social hierarchy offering some sense
of stability. For Ida, as for her mother and thousands of other
African Americans, Victorian ideals provided one escape route
from the stigma of slavery as well as from the chaos of racial
violence.[14]

The fascination in reading Wells's diary from the mid-1880s
derives in no small part from the energy and enthusiasm with

which she embraced those values. I wanted to evoke that passion for readers, whether she was playing Logomachy or watching Gilbert and Sullivan, collecting calling cards from admirers, teaching Sunday school, or mastering *Macbeth*. The consumer culture of the industrial economy was reflected too, in her constant struggle to balance the desire for clothing, furniture, or books with the need to keep her finances in order and not overextend her line of credit at Menken's ("I'm going to do a cash business after this so help me").[15] I hoped to show that cornucopia of material culture as well through some of the book's illustrations.

Wells's immersion in the consumer culture provoked conflicts as well. She cared enough about her appearance to buy a fashionable "duster" for traveling on the intercity railroad, yet encountered "the usual trouble about the first-class coach." Trade cards were hawked everywhere, including enticing portraits of *The Mikado,* yet such cards routinely employed gross racial caricatures to sell products. She read voraciously and widely, including the works of Albion Tourgee, a lawyer, civil rights activist, and novelist, yet what on earth did she make of Rider Haggard's *She,* a popular adventure novel that Wells began on Easter afternoon, 1887, in order to discover why it was "creating such a stir." Her diary never reveals whether she finished the adventures of the blond "Greek God" Leo Vincey, who journeys to a long-lost underground African kingdom ruled by a mesmerizing white goddess, Ayesha ("She Who Must Be Obeyed"). Ayesha's black subjects are kept in subjection by torturing the few who disobey her. "They are tigers to lap blood, and even now they hunger for your blood," she tells her visitors, revealing a strategy for domination not unlike that of the Ku Klux Klan. "How thinkest thou that I rule this people?

I have but a regiment of guards to do my bidding, therefore it is not by force. It is by terror." Yet in a striking reversal of roles, it is the black savages, not white mobs, who mount torchlight parades "looking like so many devils from hell" as they illuminate their rituals by burning the bodies of mummified corpses. "On rushed

UP ABOVE THEM TOWERED HIS BEAUTIFUL PALE FACE

Illustration from She, *by H. Rider Haggard*

the bearers of the flaming corpses, and . . . built their ghastly loads crossways into a huge bonfire. Heavens! how they roared and flared! No tar barrel could have burnt as did those mummies."[16]

One wonders how Wells might have reacted to this chilling inversion.

Certainly she could be contradictory, or at least unpredictable, in her adherence to middle-class values. She praised the virtues of Victorian home life in her paean of 1888, "The Model Woman: A Pen Picture of the Typical Southern Girl":

> Whatever else she may be, "the typical Southern girl" of today is not without refinement, is not coarse and rude in her manners, nor loud and fast in her deportment.
>
> Nor is the stiff, formal, haughty girl the ideal. The field is too broad and the work too great, our people are at once too hospitable and resentful to yield such one much room in their hearts.
>
> The typical girl's only wealth, in most cases, is her character; and her first consideration is to preserve that character in spotless purity.[17]

On the other hand, as biographer Linda McMurry has observed, Wells commended these ideals at the very time she was refusing to marry herself into a quiet, domestic life. Instead, she left the female profession of teaching for the largely male world of journalism, where she never shrank from controversy and debate.

Wells also extolled manhood, the Victorian counterpart to female purity. Just as black women were demeaned by racist allegations of immoral behavior, black men were denied respect by being addressed as "boy" or "uncle" rather than "Mr." or "Sir." Wells frequently urged black men to stand up for themselves. When the Tennessee Rifles guarded the Memphis jail to prevent a mob from carrying off its black prisoners, she applauded "the manhood which these Negroes represented." In discussing emigration to Oklahoma she spoke of "the chance [black settlers] had of developing manhood and womanhood in this new territory."[18]

Especially in the South, the ideal of manhood encompassed the defense of one's honor. Ruth Watkins, the white historian of Marshall County, scorned carpetbagger Nelson Gill for not fighting back when a Southern colonel pulled his beard. As for Albert McDonald, the Illinois Republican who helped found Shaw University, "No insult nor attack could arouse any anger in him whatsoever," Watkins tartly noted.[19] What sort of manhood would stand for such abuse? Perhaps ironically, Wells's instincts remained closer to the Southern honor of Watkins than to the patient pacifism of McDonald. I was struck, reading her diary, by its suggestion that a young white man's revenge killing was almost "justifiable," given the ruin of his sister's reputation.[20] Action—violent action—seemed to Wells eminently honorable. When African Americans in Kentucky set fire to white houses after a lynching, Wells hailed the news as a "true spark of manhood." In 1893, she learned that an African American who had been denied service at the Columbian World Exposition angrily "resented the manager's insulting refusal by breaking his nose and otherwise battering up his face." She "rejoice[d at the news] with all my soul."[21]

It may seem surprising that Wells would espouse such notions of honor and vengeance, but she shared those Southern values right along with those of womanhood and manhood, of middle-class consumption, and devout Christianity. Indeed, it was the combination that made her opposition to lynching so fierce.

Southern honor had put white women on a pedestal, proclaiming a reputation both pure and stainless. All her life Wells, too, understood that black women were required to preserve their own character "in spotless purity." Precisely because she believed in the ideal of the pedestal, she scorned the hypocrisy of the lyncher, who elevated white women while depriving black men of their manhood and black women of their reputations.

Honor, stainless purity, womanhood: those ideals swirled around one of the most astonishing incidents in Wells's early career, the controversy culminating in the suicide of Hattie Britton. The autobiography relates the story, but by omitting Britton's name Wells conceals how great a shock the death must have been. This omission—or as a painter might say, the silhouette of a negative space—has led Wells's two biographers to overlook the drama.[22] Wells, in her combative style, first raised the issue of black women getting jobs in return for sexual favors; then demanded that names be named. Honor required that "all forty of our public school teachers" be defended. Only after issuing that call did she discover that Hattie Britton, who taught in the classroom next to Wells's, was engaged in a liaison. Not only that, Hattie's older sister had been principal of the school where both Ida and Hattie taught, had fought for civil rights as Wells had, was known throughout the city for her concerts, and had invited Ida to her prestigious soirées. Hattie Britton's other sisters had extended a similar hospitality.

A silence remains at the center of the incident. By 1891, Wells was no longer keeping a diary. We have no idea whether she confronted Hattie over the issue. We know nothing about the relationship between Britton and the young white lawyer for the school board. Clearly though, Hattie Britton came from a talented family. Her sisters followed professional careers and her brother Thomas was a successful jockey who had just won the Tennessee Derby and who made perhaps $15,000 a year.[23] The question cannot be evaded. After the suicide, did Wells feel any regret at having publicly stirred up the issue? Did she feel responsible, even in part, for Britton's death? Or did she consider it a sadly predictable tragedy given Hattie Britton's willingness to risk her virtue in the way she did? Both Meb Britton and Wells knew "'Ostler Joe" and its familiar refrain:

'Twas the same old wretched story that for ages bards had sung,
'Twas a woman weak and wanton, and a villain's tempting
tongue.

Whatever Wells's feelings, Hattie Britton's suicide revealed how race, Victorian values, and Southern honor combined in volatile ways.

In any case, Wells had to move on. Her article criticizing the school system led to her firing, forcing her to work as a full-time journalist. Perhaps to her surprise—no doubt to her pleasure— she was able to make the *Free Speech* a thriving newspaper that served as a nerve center for social activism. One can only speculate what she might have accomplished had she been able to pursue in a sustained manner this particular line of self-definition, for she was assembling a network of correspondents as well as a subscriber base extending south into the Mississippi Delta, eastward into Tennessee, and westward into Arkansas. She was exploring ways to use the power of the press to network, to organize economic boycotts of "separate car" railroads. She was pushing African Americans at the national level to do more than make impassioned speeches.

But the social tides in the South were flowing in a different direction: toward a reconstruction of society in which race became the basis of disfranchisement and a system of segregation enforced by lynching and mob violence. For Wells, the murders of Moss, McDowell and Stewart in March 1892 proved a brutal awakening to the fact that Memphis and its more cosmopolitan world was not exempt from the "southern horrors" reported elsewhere. ("With all our proscription in theatres, hotels and on railroads, we had never had a lynching and did not believe we could have one," she wrote in 1893. "We had confidence and pride in our city and the majesty of its laws.")[24] The tragic deaths, followed three months later by Wells's exile from the world she had known, were the culmination of my story.

Yet how to tell it? The question of narrative point of view at first seemed a technical matter, easily resolved. Wells was in Natchez when the three lynchings occurred. Should I follow the Memphis story from afar, through her eyes? Clearly it made more dramatic sense to leave Wells and take up the case of the People's Grocery from Tom Moss's point of view. On the other hand, my core narrative was not about the lynchings per se. It was about the struggle of African Americans to define themselves over and against the unremitting *they says* of the culture: the continual slurs in the white press, the racist trade cards, Rider Haggard's *She,* and as always, sidewalk encounters like the one in which a black passerby was shot several days before the incident at the

Curve—ZEB NOLAN ON THE WARPATH. From the comfortable distance of the twenty-first century, it can be difficult to appreciate the drag of such prevailing winds. Even Wells, perceptive in such matters, came to understand only later how the accounts of supposed "outrages" by black men unconsciously warped her own perception of African Americans.

As I began to write, it occurred to me that an immersion in such an environment, even for a few pages, might help readers comprehend its effect more viscerally. Instead of supplying a judicious account of the riots, with the usual scholarly qualifications and judgments, why not recreate the breathless world of the Memphis papers? To do so would be disorienting, of course, especially if readers were not told at the outset whose narrative was being presented. But that was the point, in a way. Readers depend on the historian to act as an unspoken guide, to define clearly the parameters of a situation. If presented with a narrative of "turbulent and unruly negroes" rioting at the Curve, the certainties of the reader disappear. Who's talking here? Why is the language so biased? Is any of the account true? Surely some must be, or why would I be reading it? Did Moss actually shoot Cole? Where is the historian, to supply a little context?

They say. If allegations are asserted with confidence, especially by those in authority, and repeated often enough, it becomes increasingly hard not to slip one's moorings. I included only a half-dozen pages of this material, strung together chronologically from accounts in the *Memphis Appeal-Avalanche* that appeared March 6–10, 1892, but I hope it gives a sense of the crosswinds African Americans faced.[25] Then, returning home with Wells, I hoped to understand how her experience of living through the event doubly—first in the papers and second through the accounts of her friends—gave her growing insight into the dynamics of the color line. If the accounts of the Memphis lynching were so badly distorted, what of the many reports of "outrages" in other lynching cases? The Moss tragedy forced Wells to make the connections leading to her explosive editorial on consensual sex between white women and black men.

In the war of definition and self-definition, Wells's accusations were sufficient to insure banishment. Jesse Duke had been run out of Montgomery, Alabama, for his allusions to "black Romeos and white Juliets." In some ways, it is remarkable how much African Americans could say and *not* raise a mob. The editor of another Montgomery paper, in protesting lynchings, had insisted that blacks must "die like men [and]…take two or three white devils along…stop being bullied…like dogs." The *Southern Independent* in Selma predicted in 1886 that "at no distant day we will have our race war, and we hope, as God intends, that we will be strong enough to wipe you out of existence." Neither outburst provoked a hanging or an expulsion.[26] It was the mix of sex and race, rather than the threat of violence, that whites found truly incendiary. They too, after all, believed in the purity of womanhood, Southern honor, and manhood.

Lyric Hall seemed a good place to end the tale, once Wells had been exiled, for the speech she delivered that evening displayed so much of her multifaceted personality. She remained unrelenting in her opposition to lynching, yet recalled herself as being "frightened" of speaking and possessing only "some little reputation as an essayist from my schoolgirl days." Her talk evoked Tom Moss's widow as a dedicated and grieving mother, yet Wells herself continued to lead the attack on mob terror, spending her life on the lecture circuit for the greater part of three years before marrying and settling down. She was a Victorian sentimentalist, yet also a speaker who read from a written text in dispassionate tones, to prevent herself from succumbing to sentiment. She was determined to put her life in Memphis behind her, yet she wept nonetheless at Lyric Hall, pressing onward through tears.

Was I being too much of a sentimentalist myself, choosing that story as a resting place? A trained elocutionist, Wells was hardheaded enough to understand the dramatic effect of her tears. Yet they were genuine and unplanned. They arose, I believe, because despite the accolades and adulation, Wells realized her opponents had won—not only in the short run but also, likely, in the longer term. She could not see her future, but she could discern the system of segregation being shackled upon her people year by year—a system that would not be overturned until a generation after her death. For the rest of her life she assumed the formidable task of rousing whites and blacks alike to face hard truths: for whites, that racism was as pervasive in the North as in the South and would require a national solution; for blacks, that a policy of accommodation was futile so long as the color line restrained those who worked hard, did well, and "got along." For someone who perceived these truths so clearly, it was hard to sit still for accommodation, hard sometimes not to walk out in frustration or lecture her colleagues for not pushing harder.

When she came to Memphis in 1881, Ida B. Wells was not bent toward a career as an agitator. She went to church, enjoyed the theater, shopped at the department stores, sought to join in the same middle-class life that so many whites and more than a few blacks enjoyed. She was driven to her life's work because she refused to let others define her. By the time I had followed her through the twists and turns of three decades, it seemed clear enough why she acted as she did. Despite my intention to use her as an exemplar of a generation rather than as a biographical subject, I couldn't help wishing, however vainly, that I might act with half the courage and fortitude as she. I realized, with growing certainty, how much I liked her.

Selected Bibliography

Ida B. Wells

DeCosta-Willis, Miriam, ed. *The Memphis Diary of Ida B. Wells: An Intimate Portrait of the Activist as a Young Woman.* Boston: Beacon Press, 1995.

Duster, Alfreda M., ed. *Crusade for Justice: The Autobiography of Ida B. Wells.* Chicago: University of Chicago Press, 1970.

McMurry, Linda O. *To Keep the Waters Troubled: The Life of Ida B. Wells.* New York: Oxford University Press, 1998.

Royster, Jacqueline Jones, ed. *Southern Horrors and Other Writings: The Anti-Lynching Campaign of Ida B. Wells, 1892–1900.* New York: New York Age Print, 1892. Reprint. Boston: Bedford/St. Martin's, 1997.

Schechter, Patricia A. *Ida B. Wells-Barnett and American Reform, 1880–1930.* Chapel Hill: University of North Carolina Press, 2001.

Thompson, Mildred I. *Ida B. Wells-Barnett: An Exploratory Study of An American Black Woman, 1893–1930.* Brooklyn, NY: Carlson Publishing, 1990.

Holly Springs, Memphis, and the Region

Capers, Gerald M. *The Biography of a River Town: Memphis, Its Heroic Age.* Chapel Hill: University of North Carolina Press, 1939.

Cartwright, Joseph H. *The Triumph of Jim Crow: Tennessee Race Relations in the 1880s.* Knoxville: University of Tennessee Press, 1976.

Hutchins, Fred L. *What Happened in Memphis.* Kingsport, TN: Kingsport Press, 1965.

Lee, George W. *Beale Street: Where the Blues Began.* College Park, MD: McGrath Publishing Company, 1969. Reprint of 1934 edition.

Watkins, Ruth. "Reconstruction in Marshall County." *Publications of the Mississippi Historical Society* 12 (1912): 155–213.

Wharton, Vernon Lane. *The Negro in Mississippi, 1865–1890.* Studies in History and Political Science. Chapel Hill: University of North Carolina Press, 1947.

GENERAL

Ayers, Edward L. *The Promise of the New South: Life After Reconstruction.* New York: Oxford University Press, 1992.

Bederman, Gail. *Manliness and Civilization: A Cultural History of Gender and Race in the United States, 1880–1917.* Chicago: University of Chicago Press, 1995.

Edwards, Rebecca. *New Spirits: Americans in the Gilded Age, 1865–1905.* New York: Oxford University Press, 2006.

Foner, Eric. *Reconstruction: America's Unfinished Revolution, 1863–1877.* New York: Oxford University Press, 1988.

Hahn, Steven. *A Nation Under Our Feet: Black Political Struggles in the Rural South From Slavery to the Great Migration.* Cambridge, MA: Harvard University Press, 2003.

Higginbotham, Evelyn Brooks. *Righteous Discontent: The Women's Movement in the Black Baptist Church, 1880–1920.* Cambridge, MA: Harvard University Press, 1993.

Hodes, Martha. *White Women, Black Men: Illicit Sex in the Nineteenth-Century South.* New Haven: Yale University Press, 1997.

Lasch, Christopher. *Haven in a Heartless World: The Family Besieged.* New York: Basic Books, 1977.

Litwack, Leon F. *Been in the Storm So Long: The Aftermath of Slavery.* New York: Alfred A. Knopf, 1979.

Rabinowitz, Howard N. *Race Relations in the Urban South, 1865–1890.* New York: Oxford University Press, 1978.

White, Deborah Gray. *Too Heavy a Load: Black Women in Defense of Themselves, 1894–1994.* New York: W. W. Norton, 1999.

Williams, Heather Andrea. *Self-Taught: African American Education in Slavery and Freedom.* Chapel Hill: University of North Carolina Press, 2005.

Abbreviations

SH   Wells, Ida B. *Southern Horrors: Lynch Law in All Its Phases*. New York: New York Age Print, 1892. Reprint. Boston: Bedford/St. Martin's, 1997.

LL   Wells, Ida B. "Lynch Law in all Its Phases." *Our Day* 10 (May 1893), 333–337. Reprinted in Mildred I. Thompson, *Ida B. Wells-Barnett: An Exploratory Study of an American Black Woman, 1893–1930*. Brooklyn, NY: Carlson Publishing, 1990.

CJ   Wells, Ida B. *Crusade for Justice: the Autobiography of Ida B. Wells*. Alfreda M. Duster, ed. Chicago: University of Chicago Press, 1970.

McMurry   McMurry, Linda O. *To Keep the Waters Troubled: The Life of Ida B. Wells*. New York: Oxford University Press, 1998.

Diary   *The Memphis Diary of Ida B. Wells: An Intimate Portrait of the Activist as a Young Woman*. Miriam DeCosta-Willis, ed. Boston: Beacon Press, 1995.

NOTES

✵⬩⬧

PROLOGUE

1. Ofuskee County Birth Index E–F, www.rootsweb.com/okokfusk/ bdindexs/bindxef.htm. The boy was born March 16, 1911.

2. Hal Morgan and Andreas Brown, *Prairie Fires and Paper Moons: The American Photographic Postcard, 1900–1920* (Boston, 1981) provides a useful history of the postcard, upon which I have drawn. "I thought the camera could catch me," xii.

3. Accounts of the lynching from Oklahoma newspapers are quoted and summarized in James Allen, Leon Litwack, et al., *Without Sanctuary: Lynching Photography in America* (Santa Fe, NM, 2000), 178–180. It should be noted that it was relatively uncommon to see a woman lynched.

4. *The Crisis* 10 (June 1915), 71.

5. Allen et al., *Without Sanctuary*, 20–22.

6. "Southern chivalry," *Little Rock Daily News*, quoted in Allen et al., *Without Sanctuary*, 24; "brute passion," quoted in Wells, *Southern Horrors*, 63. Hereafter cited as *SH*.

7. Wells, "Lynch Law," 179. Hereafter cited as *LL*.

8. *SH*, 51–52.

9. Duster, *Crusade for Justice*, 62. Hereafter cited as *CJ*.

ONE: INTO A CHANGING WORLD

1. Watkins, "Reconstruction," 157.

2. John Eaton uses "forty-five thousand or more in Grant's command" at the time that he is moving out of Grand Junction. Quoted in Wharton, *Negro in Mississippi*, 27.

3. Hodding Carter, "A Proud Struggle for Grace: Holly Springs, Mississippi," in Thomas C. Wheeler, ed., *A Vanishing America: The Life and Times of the Small Town* (New York, 1964), 65.

4. Watkins, "Reconstruction," 157, mentions 60 raids; Carter says the town changed hands "at least 59 times." Carter, "A Proud Struggle," 64.

5. George Rawick, *The American Slave: A Composite Autobiography* (Westport, CT, 1977), Supplementary Series 1, Mississippi Narratives, vol. 6, 7, 11; Steven Hahn, *A Nation Under Our Feet: Black Political Struggles in the Rural South from Slavery to the Great Migration* (Cambridge, MA, 2003), 65; Booker T. Washington, *Up From Slavery: An Autobiography* (1901; reprint ed., New York, 1989), 7.

6. John Eaton quoted in Wharton, *Negro in Mississippi*, 28.

7. Wharton, *Negro in Mississippi*, 29–30.

8. Historic Places of Marshall County, MS, www.rootsweb.com/~msmarsha/locales/historic.html.

9. Hardwick, Kevin, "'Your old father Abe Lincoln is dead and damned': Black soldiers and the Memphis race riot of 1866," *Journal of Social History* 27 (1993), 109–122.

10. Litwack, *Been in the Storm So Long*, 170.

11. *CJ*, 8.

12. *CJ*, 10.

13. Litwack, *Been in the Storm So Long*, 240.

14. Elizabeth Avery Meriwether, *Recollections of 92 Years* (Nashville, 1958), 167; Litwack, *Been in the Storm So Long*, 258–259.

15. Litwack, *Been in the Storm So Long*, 257; Foner, *Reconstruction*, 120; John R. Dennett, *The South As It Is: 1865–1866*, ed. Henry M. Christman (New York, 1965), 42.

16. Litwack, *Been in the Storm So Long*, 256–257, 176.

17. *CJ*, 12–13.

18. George Washington Albright in Rawick, *American Slave*, Supplementary Series 1, vol. 6, 11.

19. Watkins, "Reconstruction," 174.

20. Hahn, *Nation Under Our Feet*, 185, quotes the "ring with shouts" as a response to Henry McNeal Turner reading the dialogue. For more on the League, see Michael W. Fitzgerald, *The Union League Movement in the Deep South: Politics and Agricultural Change during Reconstruction* (Baton Rouge, rev. ed., 2000).

21. Walter L. Fleming, *Documentary History of Reconstruction* (Cleveland, 1906–1907) vol. 2, 13–19.

22. Wharton, *Negro in Mississippi*, 142–143.

23. Watkins, "Reconstruction," 185; Wharton, *Negro in Mississippi*, 142–143.

24. *CJ*, 8–9.

25. Watkins, "Reconstruction," 185–186, 177; Fitzgerald, *Union League Movement*, 70. Marshall County whites also claimed that this verse of the song—a familiar one from slavery days—was followed by a new one, as the black man sharpened his knife, "Carve that white man, nigger, carve him to the heart." But whether, like some of the imagined sidewalk confrontations, this memory was exaggerated in the retelling seems difficult to know. Certainly the imagery of the possums treed was vivid enough in the first place. For the original song, see Eugene D. Genovese, *Roll, Jordan, Roll: The World the Slaves Made* (New York, 1974) 546–547. I am indebted to James E. Crisp for this reference.

26. "Satisfaction of a gentleman" is taken from another example Watkins gives of a whipping in response to an insult. Watkins, "Reconstruction," 174.

27. Watkins, "Reconstruction," 181.

28. Watkins, "Reconstruction," 175–176.

29. Allen W. Trelease, *White Terror: The Ku Klux Klan Conspiracy and Southern Reconstruction* (New York, 1971).

30. *CJ*, 9 .

31. Rawick, *American Slave,* Supplementary Series 1, vol. 6, 11–12 and vol. 8, 1155.

32. Testimony from Henry C. Myers, one of the founders of the KKK in Marshall County, in Watkins, "Reconstruction," 178.

33. Watkins, "Reconstruction," 160.

34. Watkins, "Reconstruction," 175.

35. Watkins, "Reconstruction," 180.

36. Watkins, "Reconstruction," 186–187.

37. Watkins, "Reconstruction," 177.

38. Watkins, "Reconstruction," 178.

39. Wharton, *Negro in Mississippi,* 166, on early morning voting; Watkins, "Reconstruction," 194, on Gill handing out tickets.

40. Watkins, "Reconstruction," 190.

41. Watkins, "Reconstruction," 189.

42. Wharton, *Negro in Mississippi,* 192; Foner, *Reconstruction,* 560.

43. Watkins, "Reconstruction," 184n, quoting a different Democratic black supporter.

Two: A Moral Education

1. McMurry believes that Ida attended Sunday school classes with her mother, probably at Asbury Methodist Church where Shaw classes were first held and that when she "reached her teens she enrolled in Shaw University." *McMurry,* 9–12. Clearly Ida learned to read well before she enrolled formally at Shaw, but whether that occurred in Sunday school or in some other freedman's school, like the Gills's, is not clear.

2. Heather Andrea Williams, *Self-Taught: African American Education in Slavery and Freedom* (Chapel Hill, NC, 2005), 20. Williams quotes a black minister in Kansas who explicitly says, "Knowledge is power," 75–76.

3. Williams, *Self-Taught,* 9.

4. Rawick, *American Slave,* Supplementary Series 1, vol. 6, 364.

5. Williams, *Self-Taught,* 37.

6. Watkins, "Reconstruction," 198.

7. *CJ*, 9; Williams, *Self-Taught*, 140. The teacher was in Indiana.

8. Rawick, *American Slave*, Supplementary Series 1, vol. 7, 525.

9. Carter, "Proud Struggle for Grace," 59, 71.

10. *CJ*, xv.

11. Hardwick, "'Your old father Abe Lincoln is dead and damned'" 109–122.

12. Watkins, "Reconstruction," 199.

13. Robert C. Morris, *Reading, 'Riting, and Reconstruction* (Chicago, 1976), 174–175.

14. Quoted in *McMurry*, 13. McDonald made the statement in 1875. Watkins, in typical fashion, notes that McDonald "had all the most despicable traits of the other carpetbaggers combined with an unfailing good humor. No insult nor attack could arouse any anger in him whatsoever." This, of course, is not a compliment! Watkins, "Reconstruction," 171.

15. DeCosta-Willis, *Memphis Diary*, March 11, 1886. Hereafter cited as *Diary*.

16. DeCosta-Willis in *Diary*, xxii.

17. *CJ*, 9; William D. Miller, *Mr. Crump of Memphis* (Baton Rouge, 1964), 14, speaks of the practice of popping hog bladders.

18. *Diary*, August 9, 1886.

19. Stephanie Shaw, *What a Woman Ought to Be and To Do: Black Professional Women Workers During the Jim Crow Era,* (Chicago, 1996), 14–17, 22–23; Charlotte Hawkins Brown, *The Correct Thing to Do—To Say—To Wear* (Sedalia, NC, 1940; reprinted 1995), 87–88. Other matters of etiquette have been observed in Wells's diary, such as shaking hands with her elders, November 28, 1886.

20. Frank Wilkeson in the *New York Sun*, early 1880s, quoted in Herbert Gutman, *The Black Family in Slavery and Freedom, 1750–1925* (New York, 1976), 532. It was "a hopeless task," Wilkeson concluded, "to elevate a people whose women are strumpets."

21. Shaw, *What a Woman Ought to Be*, 23–25.

22. *CJ*, 17.

23. George Knox, editor of the *Indianapolis Freeman,* (1893) quoted in *McMurry*, 55.

24. J. M. Keating, *History of the City of Memphis and Shelby County, Tennessee* (Syracuse, NY, 1888), vol. 1, 651–655.

25. Hutchins, *What Happened in Memphis*, 8.

26. Carter, "Proud Struggle for Grace," 72.

27. T. Thomas Fortune, "Ida B. Wells, A.M.," in *Women of Distinction: Remarkable in Works and Invincible in Character,* ed. Lawson V. Scruggs (Raleigh, NC, 1893), 33–39.

28. *Diary,* June 12, 1886.

THREE: UNLADYLIKE LADY

1. The connection between expulsion and the offer is my speculation. The chronology seems suggestive.

2. *CJ*, xvi; *McMurry*, 17; Schechter, *Ida B. Wells-Barnett and American Reform*, 44. Duster, in the introduction to *CJ*, suggests that Wells came to Memphis in 1882 or 1883, but McMurry places the arrival in 1881.

3. Armstead L. Robinson, "Plans Dat Comed from God: Institution Building and the Emergence of Black Leadership in Reconstruction Memphis," in *Toward a New South? Studies in Post-Civil War Southern Communities,* ed. Orville Vernon Burton and Robert C. McMath, Jr. (Westport, CT, 1982) 74, 93.

4. Robert R. Church, Sr., entry in *Tennessee Encyclopedia of History and Culture,* Tennessee Historical Society, tennesseeencyclopedia.net/image-gallery-php?EntryID=C092. Mary Church Terrell, *A Colored Woman in a White World* (Washington, DC, 1940), 7.

5. Roberta Church and Ronald Walter, *Nineteenth Century Memphis Families of Color, 1850–1900* (Memphis, 1987), chap. 2; *Diary,* August 26, September 14, 1886.

6. Hardwick, "'Your old father Abe Lincoln is dead and damned,'" 109–122.

7. Robinson, "Plans Dat Comed from God," 83–84, for a list of occupations held by blacks in Memphis, according to the 1870 city directory. My list here is a selection.

8. Beverly G. Bond, "Historic Beale Street Baptist Church," Organization of American Historians, www.oah.org/pubsnl/2003feb/bond.html.

9. Robinson, "Plans Dat Comed from God," 77, 87–93.

10. Carter, "Proud Struggle for Grace," 57; Miller, *Mr. Crump of Memphis,* 3–4.

11. Capers, *Biography of a River Town,* 221.

12. Robinson, "Plans Dat Comed from God," 84.

13. Lee, *Beale Street,* 35.

14. Linton Weeks, *Memphis: A Folk History* (Little Rock, AR, 1982), 112–114; Lee, *Beale Street,* 161; Bond, "Historic Beale Street Baptist Church."

15. Twenty-five hundred in some services in the 1870s according to Schechter, though that probably diminished as other churches hived off. Schechter, *Ida B. Wells-Barnett and American Reform,* 68.

16. Capers, *Biography of a River Town,* 231.

17. DeCosta-Willis in *Diary,* 40. McMurry argues cogently for Vance Street as Wells's home church. *McMurry,* 69.

18. Schechter delineates the CME Church (Collins Chapel) as more socially elite. Schechter, *Ida B. Wells-Barnett and American Reform,* 64–65. The Second Congregational Church is identified by DeCosta-Willis along with other churches. DeCosta-Willis in *Diary,* 47.

19. *Diary,* Moody, February 8, 1886; "white-folks Christianity," November 28, 1886; Rabbi Samfield, April 29, 1886.

20. *Diary,* February 8, 1886; January 3, 1887.

21. John H. Ellis, *Yellow Fever and Public Health in the New South* (Lexington, KY, 1992), 105; Terrell, *Colored Woman,* 38.

22. Hutchins, *What Happened in Memphis,* 23, 27.

23. *Diary,* May 23, 1886.

24. DeCosta-Willis in *Diary,* 47.

25. *Diary,* May 9, 1886.

26. *Diary,* January 21, 1886; February 8, 1886.

27. Robinson, "Plans Dat Comed from God," 83–84.

28. *New York Freeman,* December 12, 1885.

29. She notes purchasing calling cards in her diary, at a cost of 25 cents, April 24, 1887. For the preferred "Ida B. Wells," see DeCosta-Willis in *Diary,* 47; as for her title, her daughter Alfreda M. Duster noted, "Nobody except my father ever called her 'Ida.' Black women had been trying for two hundred years to be called 'Mrs.,' so it was a breach of etiquette to call her by her first name." Afterword in *Diary,* 193.

30. Hutchins, *What Happened in Memphis,* 14.

31. Ayers, *Promise of the New South,* 137.

32. Stanley J. Folmsbee, "The Origin of the First Jim Crow Law," *Journal of Southern History* (1949), 237.

33. Folmsbee, "Origin," 243.

34. Foner, *Reconstruction,* 282. But according to Howard Rabinowitz, Richmond's streetcars were not desegregated until the mid-1870s. Rabinowitz, *Race Relations,* 192.

35. Quoted in *Civil Rights Cases,* 109 U.S. 3 (1883).

36. Folmsbee, "Origin," 236–237.

37. Folmsbee, "Origin," 237. Stephen J. Riegel, "The Persistent Career of Jim Crow," *American Journal of Legal History* 28 (1984), 27. The quotation is from the *Logwood* decision of 1885 but Riegel makes it clear that this was the prevailing sentiment well before.

38. Riegel, "Persistent Career," 26.

39. Terrell, *Colored Woman,* 15–16.

40. Ayers, *Promise of the New South,* 141.

41. *McMurry,* 26; Cartwright, *Triumph of Jim Crow,* 188.

42. *Nashville American,* October 3, 5, 7, 1881; quoted in Cartwright, *Triumph of Jim Crow,* 185.

43. *McMurry,* 27.

44. Anna Julia Cooper, *A Voice from the South* (1892; reprint ed. New York, 1988), 91–92.

45. Miller, *Mr. Crump of Memphis,* 31–32.

46. *CJ,* 18–19.

47. *Ida B. Wells v. Chesapeake, Ohio & Southwestern Railroad Company,* November 4, 1884, Tennessee State Library and Archives, quoted in *McMurry,* 27.

48. *Memphis Daily Appeal,* December 25, 1884.

49. *Memphis Daily Appeal,* December 25, 1884.

50. Cartwright, *Triumph of Jim Crow,* 190–191.

51. *CJ,* 20; *Diary,* January 24, 1886.

52. *Cleveland Gazette,* December 11, 1886; *McMurry,* 51 (Froman's military service); *Diary,* April 3, May 9, 1886. Wells recorded neither the friend's name who warned her of the plot nor its details, but the outlines seem clear.

53. Nathaniel Shaler, "The Negro Problem," *Atlantic Monthly* 54 (November 1884); Gutman, *Black Family in Slavery and Freedom,* 532–537; Philip A. Bruce, *The Plantation Negro as a Freeman* (New York, 1889), 12, 17. Bruce's book was based on articles originally written for the *New York Evening Post.* See also Beverly Guy-Sheftall, *Daughters of Sorrow: Attitudes toward Black Women, 1880–1920* (Brooklyn, NY, 1990), 42.

FOUR: EDGED TOOLS

1. *Diary,* February 8, 1887.

2. "Our Women," *New York Freeman,* January 1, 1887; *CJ,* 44. Of course Wells was not strictly accurate in saying she had no brother to protect her. Both of hers were younger, however, and she had taken on the family role of protecting them, as a mother would.

3. *Diary,* October 2, 1886.

4. *Memphis Daily Appeal,* January 2, 1885, quoted in *McMurry,* 32.

5. *Diary,* March 30, May 19, December 28, 1886; August 3, 1887.

6. *Diary,* July 16, 1887.

7. *Diary,* December 29, 1885; April 11, 1887.

8. Maurice Thompson, "The Doom of Claudius and Cynthia," *Scribner's* 17:4 (February 1879), 547–552.

9. The text of the poem may be found in George R. Sims, *Ballads of Babylon* (London, 1880), 70–77.

10. *Cleveland Gazette,* April 4, 1885.

11. *Diary,* July 4, 1886; *Macbeth,* Act 5, Scene 1. Wells does not say, but I assume she gathered the speeches of Lady Macbeth into one soliloquy, unless she or some associates also played the parts of the doctor and gentlewoman watching from the shadows.

12. *Memphis Daily Appeal,* March 13, 16, 1881; Hutchins, *What Happened in Memphis,* 175–176; Schechter, *Ida B. Wells-Barnett and American Reform,* 48; McMurry, 26.

13. DeCosta-Willis in *Diary,* 35. Quoting the *Indianapolis Freeman,* December 11, 1885.

14. *New York Age,* August 11, 1888; the *Washington Bee*'s remarks, most likely written by Louis Brown, were reprinted in the *New York Freeman,* December 11, 1885.

15. *Diary,* April 20, 1886.

16. *Diary,* February 20, February 1, 1887.

17. *Diary,* December 29, 1885.

18. *Diary,* June 12, 1886; May 6, 1886; July 29, 1886.

19. *Diary,* April 29, 1886.

20. *Diary,* June 17, 1887.

21. *Diary,* December 4, February 8, 1886.

22. *Diary,* December 29, 1885; February 8, 18, 1886.

23. *Diary,* January 28, 1886.

24. *Diary,* January 21, 1886.

25. *Diary,* February 14, 1886.

26. *Diary,* August 22, 1886; April 11, 1887.

27. *Diary,* April 18, August 12, 24, 1887.

28. *Diary,* December 21, 1886.

29. *Diary,* February 14, 1886; Graham's wealth, DeCosta-Willis in *Diary,* 26.

30. *Diary,* February 8, 14, 28, 1886. For the "tight jacket," August 2, 1886.

31. *Diary,* November 28, 1886, for "ma chere ami"; February 14, 1886.

32. *Diary,* May 6, 1886. Wells, recording the line, naturally transposed it to say "he longed to sip the nectar from my curling lip."

33. *Diary,* May 6, 1886.

34. *Diary,* June 3, 1886.

35. *Diary,* June 15, 1886.

36. *Diary,* June 28, 1886.

37. *Diary,* June 28, 1886. Comments that she loves no one, is heartless, and a flirt: April 29, 1886 (Lott); June 15, 1886 (Brown and Mosely).

Five: Ambition to Edit

1. *Diary,* June 15, 1886, notes the postponement of the railroad case yet again. Wells never explicitly acknowledged using California as an escape from her perplexity over Graham and Brown, but the chronology argues strongly for it. Aunt Fannie had been pressing her to come for months, yet Wells successfully resisted until shortly after the incident in the "trysting place" with Brown. Furthermore, while living in California she confided to "Charlie Boy" Morris "of my hesitating between marrying and staying here to raise the children." She associated the option of matrimony, in other words, with Memphis, as opposed to "staying here" in Visalia and raising her sisters.

2. *Diary,* July 29, 1886.

3. *CJ,* 24–27; *Diary,* August 9, 1886.

4. *Diary,* August 9, 1886.

5. *Diary,* September 12, October 20, 1886.

6. Some historians date the article (copies of which have not survived) to 1883. According to the Goodspeed Publishing Company's *History of Tennessee from the Earliest Times…* (Nashville, 1887), 908, the *Living Way* began publication February 10, 1884, from offices at 161 Beale Street.

7. *Diary,* March 11, 1886; *McMurry,* 90.

8. Firm numbers have been very difficult to determine because black newspapers regularly went in and out of business. I. Garland Penn, *The Afro-American Press and Its Editors* (Springfield, MA, 1891), the classic contemporary study, provided an estimate of one hundred fifty papers in 1890 but surely undercounted. Georgia Merritt Campbell, *Extant Collections of Early Black Newspapers: A Research Guide to the Black Press, 1880–1915 with an Index to the Boston Guardian 1902–1904* (Troy, NY, 1981) discovered more than 1,876 during the period she catalogued. The most extensive survey is James P. Danky, ed., *African-American Newspapers and Periodicals: A National Bibliography* (Cambridge, MA, 1998). See also Henry Louis Suggs, ed., *The Black Press in the South, 1865–1979* (Westport, CT, 1983) and Julius Eric Thompson, *The Black Press in Mississippi, 1865–1985* (West Cornwall, CT, 1988).

9. *Indianapolis Freeman,* January 7, 1891.

10. *Diary,* March 1, 1886.

11. "Honey and stings" quoted in *McMurry*, 91; *Cleveland Gazette,* September 18, 1886.

12. *Diary,* December 29, 1885; February 18, 25, 1886.

13. For a good survey of the topic, see Rodger Streithammer, *Raising Her Voice: African-American Women Journalists Who Changed History* (Lexington, KY, 1993); 47 for Mossell's income.

14. "Women's Mission," *New York Freeman,* December 26, 1885; "The Model Woman," *New York Freeman,* February 18, 1888. Another example is "Our Women," a letter to the *Memphis Scimitar* reprinted by the *New York Freeman,* January 1, 1887. All are reprinted in *Diary*.

15. *Cleveland Gazette,* July 6, 1889.

16. For examples of such concerns, randomly chosen for this paragraph and the previous one, see the *Cleveland Gazette,* September 18, 1886, January 29, 1887.

17. "A Word Concerning Our Southern Editors," reprinted in the *New York Freeman* of February 7, 1885, featured the pen name of "Iola."

18. *Diary,* June 28, 1886.

19. Wells, "Functions of Leadership," *Living Way,* September 12, 1885, reprinted in *Diary,* 179.

20. Rabinowitz, *Race Relations in the Urban South*, 195.

21. Wells, "Iola on Discrimination," *New York Freedman,* January 15, 1887, reprinted in *Diary,* 186–187.

22. *Diary,* January 5, 28 and March 11, 18, 1886.

23. *McMurry,* 93, makes the astute inference that Wells had been complaining about journalists' pay in the *Living Way,* although the article or articles that offended Chase have not survived; certainly Wells's diary supports the inference, for her requests for pay occur at about this time.

24. *Diary,* February 18, 1886.

25. *CJ,* 32, suggests that Simmons immediately offered Wells a dollar an article and that she had never before thought of being paid for her work. But the diary makes clear that she had been asking for pay and that at first, Simmons reimbursed her by sending extra copies of his magazine. *Diary,* November 7, 15, 1886; the contract is mentioned January 18, 1887.

26. *Diary,* August 12, 17, 24, 1887.

27. *New Orleans Weekly Pelican,* quoted in *McMurry,* 99.

28. *Indianapolis Freedman,* February 23, 1889, quoted in *CJ,* 33.

29. Cartwright, *Triumph of Jim Crow,* 55.

30. Cartwright, *Triumph of Jim Crow,* 137–141; Schechter, *Ida B. Wells-Barnett and American Reform,* 39–41.

31. *Chesapeake, Ohio and S. W. Railroad v. Ida Wells,* April 1885, quoted in Cartwright, *Triumph of Jim Crow,* 191. It was not unusual for whites to denigrate legal suits by blacks. The *New York Times* commented in June 1874, that whenever African Americans believed "their rights are assailed or threatened, a rush is made to some court or other for redress." Quoted in Riegel, "Persistent Career of Jim Crow," 22.

32. *Diary,* April 11, 1887.

33. *Memphis Avalanche,* January 26, 1890; quoted in Cartwright, *Triumph of Jim Crow,* 181.

34. Cartwright, from whom I have taken these quoted sentiments, details the shifting progression toward segregation with sensitivity. Cartwright, *Triumph of Jim Crow,* 45–46, 181, 178.

35. *Diary,* November 9, 1889; Cartwright, *Triumph of Jim Crow,* 144, 240.

36. The Will Lewis incident is described in *SH,* 60.

37. *Diary,* April 18, 1887.

38. *McMurry,* 121.

39. Ayers, *Promise of the New South,* 50–51; Cartwright, *Triumph of Jim Crow,* 52–56, 239–247.

40. *Cleveland Gazette,* August 4, 1888. After a period of transition, the *Free Speech and Headlight* changed its name to the *Free Speech.*

41. Wells quotes Duke in *SH,* 53; see also Allen W. Jones, "The Black Press in the 'New South': Jesse C. Duke's Struggle For Justice and Equality," *Journal of Negro History* 64, no. 3 (1979), 215–228.

42. Cartwright, *Triumph of Jim Crow,* 175. Reported in the *Knoxville Journal,* June 27, 1889. There is no indication whether the group pursued this strategy of embarrassment.

43. *Free Speech,* quoted (disapprovingly) in the *Memphis Weekly Avalanche,* June 13, 1889.

44. *Detroit Plaindealer,* October 18, 1889.

45. Wells, "A Story of 1900," *Fisk Herald,* April 1886, reprinted in *Diary,* 182–184.

46. *CJ,* 36. It is worth noting that the relevant issues of the *Free Speech* have not survived—nor any issues, for that matter—only excerpts quoted in other papers. Wells's language here is from her autobiography. I discuss the evidence for this reconstruction in the afterword.

47. W. D. Johnson, *Biographical Sketches of Prominent Negro Men and Women of Kentucky* (Lexington, KY, 1897), entry for Benjamin Franklin, Susan's husband. See also, under the entry for Franklin, *Notable Kentucky African Americans,* University of Kentucky, www.uky.edu/Subject/aakyall.html.

48. *Diary,* August 17, 24; September 6, 1887.

49. *Detroit Plaindealer,* June 12, 1891; *CJ,* 36–37. For the Lauderdale Street residence, see DeCosta-Willis in *Diary,* 54.

50. The reason for Nightingale's dispute is unclear. Church records throughout the centuries are replete with such quarrels, and this was yet another. In addition, however, many whites in Memphis assumed that Nightingale had written some of the *Free Speech*'s outspoken articles. They may have used the dispute to their advantage by trumping up assault charges when Nightingale physically tried to bar some members from entering the church. When convicted, he fled to Oklahoma rather than serve his sentence in the Shelby County workhouse. See David M. Tucker, *Black Pastors and Leaders: Memphis 1819—1972* (Memphis, TN, 1975), 45–46; also *McMurry*, 129.

51. *CJ,* 39–42.

52. *Cleveland Gazette,* August 1, 1891.

53. *Memphis Weekly Avalanche,* September 6, 1891, quoting the *Free Speech*. The *New York Times* reported the story on August 30.

SIX: THEY SAY

1. The language in this chapter is taken nearly verbatim from accounts in the *Memphis Appeal-Avalanche* of March 6–11, 1892, though the narrative has been condensed. The spelling, capitalization, and punctuation of the original have been retained. I discuss the treatment of this material in the afterword.

SEVEN: DO SOMETHING

1. *CJ,* 47–48.

2. Ayers, *Promise of the New South,* 85.

3. Wells, "Lynch Law in all Its Phases," 173. Hereafter cited as *LL.*

4. *McMurry*, 130; Hutchins, *What Happened in Memphis,* 37.

5. *Detroit Plaindealer,* April 1, 1892.

6. *St. Paul Appeal,* March 26, 1892. The *Appeal* printed a statement from five Memphis ministers, including R. N. Countee, the former editor of the *Living Way.* Designed both to counter the rabid accounts in the white Memphis dailies as well as to calm the unsettled situation in Memphis, the statement provides perhaps the best single account of the troubles leading up to the lynching. Wells's account in *LL,* though written more than a year after the event, contains many useful details.

7. *Memphis Appeal-Avalanche,* March 2, 1892.

8. David M. Tucker, "Miss Ida B. Wells and Memphis Lynching," *Phylon* 33, no. 2 (1971), 115. See also the *Memphis Appeal-Avalanche,* March 8, 1892.

9. *St. Paul Appeal,* March 26, 1892; for Barrett's role see also the *Detroit Plaindealer,* March 18, 1992, the *Cleveland Gazette,* March 19, 1892, and *LL,* 174.

10. According to some accounts, Thomas Moss and his wife Betty both claimed, at different times, that he was not at the grocery that evening. (See for example Hutchins, a historian with strong roots in the Memphis community, *What Happened in Memphis,* 37.) On the other hand, the contemporary statement of black ministers in the *St. Paul Appeal* places Moss at the store reading a paper when the deputies entered. Given Moss's usual behavior, which was to come in evenings, and given the threat of a mob, it would seem likely that he was on hand. Even if he had been working all day Saturday, at the time when Barrett conveyed the threat, McDowell or Stewart surely would have sent word to his house.

11. *CJ,* 50n. The recollection cited suggests that the Rifles guarded the jail for three nights, so perhaps the militia scrambled quickly enough to put someone in place early Sunday morning, after McDowell and others were taken to the jail. But the Rifles clearly had withdrawn, or been ordered withdrawn, by Tuesday night.

12. *Cleveland Gazette,* April 4, 1892. The exact chronology of DuBose's order and the disarming of the Tennessee Rifles is unclear from the conflicting or vague accounts. Another possibility is that the order may have come the day after the lynching.

13. *LL,* 174.

14. *Memphis Commercial,* March 10, 1892; *CJ,* 50–51; *LL,* 175; *Memphis Appeal-Avalanche,* March 10, 1892.

15. *Cleveland Gazette,* March 18, 1892. Wells's autobiography and *LL* place this looting on Wednesday, March 9, after DuBose sent out his armed force, which makes sense, though the *Gazette's* report specifically mentions the Sabbath. Between newspaper reports, which were often garbled, and later recollections, which are often inexact, it is difficult to place all of these actions with certainty. See also the *Memphis Appeal-Avalanche,* March 10,

1892; Hutchins, *What Happened in Memphis*, 38. For the supplies sold to Barrett, *LL*, 179–180.

16. *Detroit Plaindealer*, March 18, 1892. Wells quoted in *McMurry*, 140.

17. *CJ*, 62.

18. Hutchins, *What Happened in Memphis*, 38–39; the *Memphis Appeal-Avalanche*, March 8, 1892, also makes mention of closing a powder magazine whose owner was accused of supplying blacks.

19. Quoted in *CJ*, 52.

20. *Memphis Appeal-Avalanche*, March 22, 1892.

21. Tucker, "Miss Ida B. Wells and Memphis Lynching," 116n.

22. Quoted in *McMurry*, 142.

23. *CJ*, 53–55.

24. *LL*, 179.

25. Quoted in *CJ*, 57.

26. Wells gives the higher figure, "nearly" six thousand, *LL*, 177. Four thousand is more commonly mentioned. The population of Memphis in 1890 was approximately sixty-four thousand. Capers, *Biography of a River Town*, 205.

27. *New York Age*, August 11, 1888.

28. *LL*, 172.

29. *Memphis Commercial*, May 17, 1892, quoted in *SH*, 62.

30. *SH*, 57; *CJ*, 65.

31. *SH*, 55–56.

32. Quoted in *SH*, 80.

33. *SH*, 51–52.

34. *SH*, 52.

35. *LL*, 179.

36. *CJ*, 61. The autobiography mentions Jersey City as the rendezvous, though *LL*, written closer to the event, speaks of "landing in" New York. I assume she met Fortune in New Jersey and they took a ferry across.

EIGHT: EXILED

1. *Trow's New York City Directory*, vol. 103 (New York, 1889), 1226. Lyric Hall was located at 723 Sixth Avenue.

2. *St. Paul Appeal*, August 10, 1892; *LL*, 179–180.

3. *CJ*, 63.

4. *New York Times*, February 22, 1892.

5. *SH*, 70, 61; *LL*, 182.

6. *SH*, 57.

7. It is impossible, of course, to discern the old man's motives in making such a comment. Did he condemn the young black woman only to please the white reporter? According to the article, the mob was still assembled when the comment was made. (Coy's body was said to be still "writhing" atop the bonfire.) Was the old man trying to protect the young black woman from becoming another lynch victim after she spoke out so forthrightly against the cruelty of the burning? For that matter, given the ease with which reporters of the era concocted dramatic stories, was this convenient editorial reaction made up?

8. *CJ*, 136, (Bishop Fitzgerald), 72.

9. *CJ*, 71.

10. Quoted in Gutman, *Black Family in Slavery and Freedom*, 538–539. The conference was held at a resort in the Catskill Mountains of New York in 1890 and was attended as well by former president Rutherford B. Hayes.

11. *CJ*, 90–113; 135–137; 143–223.

12. In Britain, *SH* was issued under the title *U.S. Atrocities*. The quotation from the *London Sun* was reprinted in the *Memphis Appeal-Avalanche*, June 12, 1894.

13. Linda McMurry assembled many of these unflattering characterizations (and a few more), noting that they appeared within a single choleric article in the *Memphis Commercial* of May 26, 1892. *McMurry*, 214. Other Memphis papers were critical as well.

14. *CJ*, 214.

15. *CJ*, 84, 149.

16. *CJ,* 182.

17. *CJ,* 218n for "mulatress missionary"; for a few examples of disapproval, see the *New York Times,* October 31, 1895; December 1, 1895; for coverage of Wells's antilynching efforts, see July 30, September 4, and December 11, 1894.

18. *CJ,* 235.

19. Tucker, "Miss Ida B. Wells and Memphis Lynching," 121.

20. *St. Paul Appeal,* October 21, 1899.

21. *McMurry,* 251.

22. *Topeka Weekly Call,* July 15, 1893; *CJ,* 118–119.

23. Both comments quoted in *McMurry,* 282, 213.

24. *CJ,* 286 ("besetting sin"); *Diary,* December 29, 1885; March 1, 1887; January 3, 1887.

25. *CJ,* 228–230.

26. *LL,* 172–173.

27. "Lynching: Our National Crime," *Proceedings of the National Negro Conference 1909: New York, May 31 and June 1* (n.p., n.d.), 174–179, quoted in *McMurry,* 280.

28. I am indebted to McMurry's insightful analysis of the underlying conflicts between Wells's radicalism and the accommodationism of Washington, and Wells's radicalism and the reformist positions of Susan Anthony. To an even greater extent, the same dynamic operated with reformer Frances Willard of the Woman's Christian Temperance Union, who clashed with Wells in similar ways. See *McMurry,* 256 (on Washington) and 213 (on Willard, though the same analysis works in terms of Anthony's less racist but nonetheless more hopeful notion of the elevating effects of women's purity if they won the vote).

29. See the prologue.

30. *CJ,* 3.

31. The words are taken from *Diary,* February 14, 1887, a characteristic thought.

32. "Her quiet, refined manner, her intelligence and earnestness, her avoidance of all oratorical tricks and her dependence upon the simple

eloquence of facts make her a powerful and convincing advocate." The *Guardian* (Manchester) quoted in the *Memphis Appeal-Avalanche,* May 23, 1893. "Unimpassioned agitator," a Liverpool minister, quoted in *CJ,* 146–147.

33. *SH,* 60.

34. *LL,* 172. The text is from the speech as delivered in Boston on February 13, 1893, but Wells made clear that this was essentially the same speech given in New York, though modified to include more recent events. *CJ,* 82.

35. *CJ,* 79–80.

36. *Diary,* April 11, 1887.

AFTERWORD

1. Allen et al., *Without Sanctuary*, plate 48 (Cairo, Illinois), "real photo postcard," 204.

2. Allen et al., *Without Sanctuary,* plates 25, 26. May 16, 1916, Waco, Texas.

3. Kimberly W. Benston kindly set me straight about Baldwin's original wording, which can be found in "A Talk to Teachers," James Baldwin, *The Price of the Ticket* (New York, 1985), 325–332.

4. Barbara J. Fields reports this instructive but "probably apocryphal" story in "Ideology and Race in American History," in J. Morgan Kousser and James M. McPherson, eds., *Region, Race, and Reconstruction: Essays in Honor of C. Vann Woodward* (New York, 1982), 146.

5. In 2005, scientists announced that they had discovered the genetic location of a mutation that produced a lighter skin in humans tens of thousands of years ago. The mutation, affecting only a tiny portion of the human genetic code, reinforced the notion that "almost all the differences used to differentiate populations from around the world really are skin deep." *Washington Post,* December 15, 2005; *Science* 310 (December 16, 2005), 1782–86.

6. *CJ,* 270.

7. She did enrage some readers by remarking once that if she had any blood to be ashamed of, it was her white blood, given the crimes of white civilization.

8. *McMurry*, 11, "race man"; critical of well-to-do African Americans, "Functions of Leadership," reprinted in *Diary*, 179; Shaw, *What a Woman Ought to Be*, 55.

9. Hodes, *White Women, Black Men*, 157–158.

10. Hodes, *White Women, Black Men*, 153; *McMurry*, 237.

11. James E. Crisp, *Sleuthing the Alamo: Davy Crockett's Last Stand and Other Mysteries of the Texas Revolution* (New York 2005), 13.

12. Watkins, "Reconstruction," 187, 169.

13. Terrell, *Colored Woman*, 1–2.

14. Several useful studies, among the many that touch on Victorianism are Christopher Lasch, *Haven in a Heartless World: the Family Besieged* (New York 1977); Edwards, *New Spirits*; Bederman, *Manliness and Civilization*.

15. *Diary*, March 20, 1887.

16. H. Rider Haggard, *She: A History of Adventure* (London, 1887; reprinted 1927), 182, 222–223.

17. Ida B. Wells, "The Model Woman: A Pen Picture of the Typical Southern Girl," *New York Freeman*, February 18, 1888, reprinted in *Diary*, 188.

18. *CJ*, 50, 58.

19. Watkins, "Reconstruction," 170. Watkins also reported that "two young men" once tried to provoke McDonald "to some statement or act for which they could horsewhip him. They even tore off part of his coat-tail, but seemingly he resented none of their taunts nor insults," 188–189.

20. See chapter 4.

21. *Memphis Weekly Avalanche*, September 6, 1891, quoting the *Free Speech*; Schechter, *Ida Wells-Barnett and American Reform*, 96.

22. McMurry, who is invariably astute in analyzing Wells's personality, makes no mention of the Britton suicide, related in the autobiography. Patricia Schechter does discuss it, and it was her keen eye that spotted the brief entry in the *Detroit Plaindealer* identifying Britton. Yet Schechter minimizes the suicide's connection to Britton's liaison, commenting (though without any evidence) that "much more must have been

operating in Britton's life to prompt this desperate act." Schechter, *Ida Wells-Barnett and American Reform*, 72. It seems to me that in an era when respectable black women needed to guard their reputations for "spotless purity" at all costs, it is hardly clear that "much more must have been operating" to provoke suicide. Schechter further suggests that Wells "likely spoke out in frustration *after* the sensational suicide" (my emphasis). The autobiography, however, explicitly states that Wells happened upon Britton's liaison "not long after" her article had "created a sensation" and after her paper "made rejoinder demanding the names of such teachers." The autobiography was written nearly forty years later, of course; conceivably Wells misremembered the sequence of events. (Elsewhere she occasionally confuses dates.) That would only make her actions more problematic, however, for then she would have known Hattie Britton was having an affair before she demanded that names be published. Furthermore, Wells's complaint was that these young teachers were unqualified. Because Hattie Britton came from a talented family, she most likely was reasonably well suited for her job. Selma S. Lewis and Marjean G. Kremer refer to the suicide in their fictionalized biography of Julia Britton Hooks, but the authors seem unaware of Hattie's existence, or that she was staying with Julia, referring to the suicide as "that woman" who had taught at Clay Street School. Selma S. Lewis and Marjean G. Kremer, *The Angel of Beale Street* (Memphis, 1986), 268.

23. *Detroit Plaindealer,* June 12, 1891; Lewis and Kremer, *Angel of Beale Street,* 223. The *Cleveland Gazette* reported Thomas Britton's victory and salary, June 13, 1891.

24. *LL,* 173.

25. It may be worth a few further words about the method used to create the prose narrative of chapter 6. To begin, I transcribed the coverage from one newspaper, the *Memphis Appeal-Avalanche,* in the original issues of March 6–10, 1892. With that draft in hand, I condensed the narrative to a more manageable length. Occasionally I made minor changes in punctuation for reasons of clarity. Even more rarely I broke up a sentence or added a conjunction or connective phrase. I deliberately retained the paper's stylistic conventions, including the use of the lowercase "negro." In terms of introducing bias, of course, it can be argued that any degree of selection creates a partial view. I did omit some longer descriptive

passages, such as an extended retelling of the mob's hunt for the jail-cell keys in the March 9 issue. But I believe that the selection presented in chapter 6 provides an accurate sample of the newspaper coverage in the local white press, including its many confident yet false assertions and its contradictory evidence.

26. Jones, "Black Press in the 'New South,'" 219, 220.

ILLUSTRATION CREDITS

2–3 Courtesy of the Allen-Littlefield Collection; 4 Collection of the author; 4 Collection of the author; 6 Courtesy of the Allen-Littlefield Collection; 17 Ida B. Wells-Barnett Museum, Holly Springs, MS; 24 Library of Congress, cph 3b44035; 29 Louisiana State University at Shreveport, Noel Memorial Library, Archives and Special Collections; 37 Library of Congress, cph 3c11152; 38 Matthew Simpson, *Cyclopaedia of Methodism* [Philadelphia, 1878]. Yale University, Divinity School Library; 40 Collection of the author; 52 University of Chicago Library, Department of Special Collections; 57 Memphis and Shelby County Room, Memphis Public Library; 59 Thomas Oscar Fuller, *Pictorial History of the American Negro* [1933]; Collection of American Literature; Beinecke Rare Book and Manuscript Library; 63 Collection of the author; 78 (left) Library of Congress, LC-DIG-ppmsca-04800; (right) Courtesy of the Rare Book, Manuscript, and Special Collections Library, Duke University; 81 Library of Congress, Collection of Music, Theater and Dance; 83 Courtesy of the Missouri Historic Costume Collection, Department of Textile and

Apparel Management, University of Missouri–Columbia; 84 (left) Hooks Brothers Photo/Press-Scimitar Morgue Files/Special Collections, University of Memphis Libraries; (right) Library of Congress; 101 State Archives of Florida; 104 Library of Congress; 120 Tench Coxe Collection, Bundle #1 coxerr002a, D.H. Ramsey Library Special Collections, UNC Asheville 28804; 138 Library of Congress; 141 Library of Congress; 147 Library of Congress; 149 University of Chicago Library, Department of Special Collections; 160 Library of Congress, LC-USZ62-107756; 164 Library of Congress; 170 University of Chicago Library, Department of Special Collections; 188 Farm Security Administration, Library of Congress, LC-USF34-52631-D; 194 Vassar College Libraries

INDEX